LIFE IN REGENCY YORK: 1811 to 1820

To my cousin Lesley George

Front Cover: *A young lady in a Regency gown from the Costume Gallery at York Castle Museum (by their kind permission; photograph Prudence Bebb).*

Back Cover: *Blue Coat Schoolboy depicted in St Helen's Church window (by their kind permission; Photograph by Peter Gibson MBE, York Glaziers Trust).*

ISBN 1 85072 095 9

The author wishes to express her thanks for the co-operation of York Reference Library; The York Castle Museum; Regimental Museum of the Prince of Wales' Own Regiment of Yorkshire; The National Army Museum; Upper Poppleton Library.

She appreciates very greatly grants from various trusts who wish to remain anonymous, as well as loan assistance from The Oliver Sheldon Trust.

She is also deeply grateful for the support of her mother, Mrs Elsie Bebb and her friend, Mrs Estra Clark.

Printed in 10 on 11 point Bembo Typeface
by William Sessions Limited
The Ebor Press, York, England
Successors to William Alexander of Castlegate, York

Life in
REGENCY
YORK

1811~1820

Prudence Bebb, BA

Sessions Book Trust
York, England

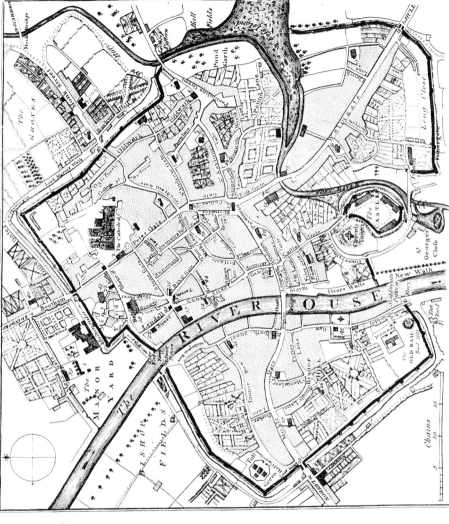

York by William Harrow 1818

Contents

Illustrations

The Regency

OLD HISTORY BOOKS MAY STILL be found which say that George III went mad; he didn't. He was the victim of a disease, porphyria, which has only been diagnosed in recent years. There was no effective remedy for his condition and it affected the mental processes. He was a kindly, popular, high-principled (although stubborn) monarch; nevertheless, a man who tries to run a race with a horse and mistakes one of the trees in Windsor Great Park for a German king cannot be said to be capable of fulfilling the constitutional duties of Britain's sovereign. Parliament was compelled to appoint someone to do his work and, with some reluctance, gave the task to his expensive and emotionally unstable eldest son – also called George but 'Prinny' to his friends.

Prinny was not without his good points. His artistic flair encouraged a blossoming of architecture and allied arts so that this period is universally recognised as deserving the accolade for elegance and good taste.

It is equally famous for its military history. When the Prince of Wales became Regent, Napoleon had conquered, or forced into alliance with France, all Europe from the Atlantic breakers to the Russian snows with the exception of the Turkish lands and Portugal. The British Army was in the Peninsula assisting the Spaniards in their revolt against the French Emperor (usually referred to in England as Boney or The Monster).

Jane Austen's *Sense and Sensibility* was being published in the year the Regency began and two of her brothers were in 'Nelson's Navy' fighting the French. Small children were labouring long hours in textile factories and the elderly poor were ending their lives in workhouses. New crops and herds were introduced to the English countryside where open fields, shared by peasants, were fast being turned into neatly enclosed farms creating rich landowners and landless labourers. It was the age of classical furniture, capital punishment and coaching inns – an age of variety, prosperity and a confidence which amounted at times to jingoism.

In this book we look at York people and what they were doing during those nine famous years, from 1811 to 1820.

Last Stage, York

The outside passenger on the London stage must have relaxed with relief when the coach approached York; he would have been travelling for 29½ hours. The road from Selby was muddy and rough by turns so the stage had to swing north-westwards at Doncaster and was approaching the city of York by the Tadcaster road.

As it drew level with the windmill whose memory is perpetuated in Mill Mount, the weary traveller couldn't hear the swish of the gyrating sails or the banging of the quants because of the rattling and thudding of the High-Flyer or the Wellington on which he sat, but he could see Micklegate Bar ahead.

Open countryside was giving place to the first houses, some of these may still be seen today beside the cobbles in Blossom Street. A blow of the guard's horn probably heralded their arrival as the coach passed the Bar Convent on the right and the Windmill Inn on the left. The Windmill had stabling for 60 horses but there was a cottage beside it and a narrow lane where the present Queen Street leads to the station.

Micklegate Bar itself was in need of repair. It still had its barbican (like Walmgate today) but there were signs that this would soon have to be demolished. With a metallic ring of the horses' hooves, the great ton-weight of the coach entered the old city, whilst the roof passenger instinctively ducked his head under the arch.

On the passenger's right was the stone priory gateway flanked by ancient overhanging houses; on his left were elegant modern residences. But this was 1811, the year that George III had sunk into a twilight of hallucinations and his son had become the Prince Regent, so 'modern' meant tall brick façades punctuated by sash windows and a door with a fanlight.

As the coach lumbered down the steep hill, the guard probably jumped from the dicky seat to place a skid on the wheel; this was an iron shoe which acted as a brake.

When the steaming team reached the bottom of the hill, they clattered over the only bridge which spanned the cold grey waters of the Ouse, then passed the timbered buildings of Ousegate. Here it might narrowly miss children sitting on the uneven ground and itinerant tradesmen calling for

The Black Swan, Coney Street.

custom : milk fresh from the cow, knives to grind. At least there ought not to be an unattended waggon or carriage. If you left horses and a vehicle whilst you wandered off shopping, you could be fined five shillings – and that was a lot of money (about half a week's wages for a labourer in Regency England) but a special Act of Parliament had decreed this penalty to improve the safety of York's streets.

At this point the outside passenger may have glanced towards the right in the direction of the slums but the coach would sweep left round the corner into Spurriergate. If it was the High-Flyer it was making for Etteridge's Hotel nearly opposite the present Public Library. If it was the Wellington, its destination was the Black Swan or the York Tavern depending which day of the week it was.

We'll take our hypothetical traveller to the York Tavern as he clutches the roof rail and looks with tired eyes at the buildings in Coney Street.

On his right the classical façade of the Black Swan was enlivened by a large replica of that bird with outstretched wings. In contrast, the George Inn farther down on the other side, had an ornately carved medieval frontage. From his position on the coach roof the traveller could see more than the inside passengers could; he was able to look through the inn doorway and see a vaulted roof over the stone passage. A pillar from the entrance to the George still stands in Coney Street embedded in the wall near the store called Next.

3

The Naval Officer.

His advantageous position also gave our passenger a unique view of the church clock of St Martin-le-Grand. He could see that this clock, overhanging the street on a bracket, was surmounted by the figure of a naval officer in blue coat and white small clothes levelling his sextant at the sun. The traveller from London would have seen men like him coming out of the Admiralty with orders to seek Napoleon's ships and destroy them. Today the blue-coated figure still stands on his bracket looking into the distance. He has survived the bombing of a later and more terrible war when St Martin-le-Grand was struck in an air raid.

The coachman would be slowing his horses as they approached the Mansion House. The equipage, its gaudy colours dulled by mud or dust according to the weather, turned into St Helen's Square. The time was half-past four in the afternoon, unless they were late, and they'd been 'on the go' since they'd left London at eleven the previous morning. Journey's end was the wide brick façade of the York Tavern on the site where Betty's is today.

The guard would produce a ladder and the roof passenger descended stiffly to all the bustle of a busy inn with its cries of 'Ostler!', 'Waiter!' He would see a bowing landlord, a scurrying maid, the cold stand with its huge cheeses and its veal and ham pies. He could smell sizzling steaks and frying bacon which mingled with beeswax, leather and horses. His exhausted mind could turn to home-brewed ale, imported wines and smuggled brandy. Yorkshire accents reached him from the coffee room as he ordered mutton collops. Soon his aching body would find the comfort of a four-poster bed, its feather mattress warmed by hot cinders in a copper warming-pan.

Nearby the Minster brooded over a city of medieval streets and the London traveller had reached his destination hoping he would not be treated as the 'outsider' he had been throughout his journey.

Naturally, not everyone came to York on the stage. If you were in a hurry and willing to travel at night, the mail coach was the answer. These great red and black vehicles all left the GPO in London between 6 and 8 p.m. according to the distance they had to travel; York's went at 7.30. The intrepid traveller paid more for a seat but felt safer because the scarlet-coated guard was armed with a blunderbuss, two pistols and permission to

4

shoot. It was only a foolhardy highwayman who attempted to rob the mail.

Darkness had fallen again by the time you entered York for the mail was due at the York Tavern at eight o'clock but, if it was winter, bell-shaped lamps were casting a yellow glow over the pavements. As you rolled down Coney Street past the milliner's and the music warehouse, you'd get your purse to tip the guard who had looked after your gold watch and any other valuables on the journey. He was probably expecting half-a-crown, a useful addition to his half-guinea weekly wage.

York's GPO was a different building from the present one but still near the junction of Lendal and St Helen's Square. Here the guard would jump down and unlock the trap door, where his feet had rested during the journey, to lift out the sacks of mail which he had guarded literally with his life.

York's citizens knew this and responded generously when the *York Chronicle* appealed: 'To the Charitable and Humane, William Redford, Mail Guard, whose death (occasioned by a fall from the mail box) was lately made known in the papers, conducted himself in his business for ten years with the strictest attention, exactness and propriety . . . About two years ago, in consequence of the bursting of his blunderbuss, his left hand was so dreadfully shattered as to render amputation necessary . . .' The paper asked for subscriptions on behalf of his widow and children to be taken to one of the York banks, the Post Office or the various coachmen and innkeepers who were collecting.

The Edinburgh Mail Coach in front of the Mansion House.

5

Complaints had been made that the York-Edinburgh mail was more overloaded with parcels on the roof than any other mail coach in the kingdom with the eventual result that it overturned and killed someone. Undoubtedly we should have been relieved to reach our destination whole if we had travelled to York in the Regency years.

We should also have found a York much smaller and rather different from the present town. Almost all of it was situated inside the city walls and most streets followed the same plan that they do today but there were three big differences.

The large space of Parliament Street, familiar to modern tourists, simply didn't exist but Jubbergate (where they collected donations for the mail guard's widow at the Black Dog) started in the present market and extended to Coney Street; its lower reach is named Market Street today. Its centre stretch was bordered by old houses and shops with their courtyards, stables and outbuildings.

Similarly there was no Piccadilly; the Pavement (which runs past Marks and Spencer's clothes store) continued until it met the junction of Ousegate and Coppergate by the 'lantern church'. Now if you look at 'Duttons for Buttons' you see a typical building of the type which once

Jubbergate

6

covered the pedestrian crossing and traffic lights of modern Piccadilly. There was a market cross here and traders sold food on Tuesdays, Thursdays and Saturdays. Henry Cave, an artist who lived in Regency times, has left us a busy-looking picture of the Pavement when the church of St Crux still stood there and market carts rumbled over the uneven road. Georgian façades mingle with overhanging houses like those still visible in the Shambles. Gossips, beggars, shoppers and tradesmen listen to the latest news.

But perhaps the biggest difference between modern and Regency York was near to Clifford's Tower.

Today the visitor arriving by the A19 must choose his traffic stream carefully as he approaches Castle Mills Bridge because he could be turning right at the traffic lights, making for the hotel and the Castle Museum. The Regency visitor from Selby was probably on horseback because the road was not turnpiked, so carriages or waggons might find it impassable in places. Castle Mills Bridge had recently been rebuilt but there was no Skeldergate Bridge; anyone wanting to cross the Ouse there had to use the ferry.

On the rider's left was St George's Field, green and damp; on his right the Law Courts were less obvious than today because a high wall

The Pavement

7

Castlegate Postern Lane.

surrounded the castle precincts. A lane skirted the wall and the visitor had to go through a narrow gateway known as Castlegate Postern. The horseman would have to guide his mount carefully to avoid the post erected on the stony lane in the centre of the archway. It prevented the illegal entrance of heavy vehicles. Hay wains, family coaches, cartloads of logs – all these types of transport would have to enter the city from Micklegate and the Tadcaster road or Monkgate and the Bridlington route. However, a light carriage could come in provided the gate-keeper used the key (officially in the custody of an Alderman) to lower the post.

If you could be transported back in time to Regency York, this is an area which you would hardly recognise. To begin with, you'd find that the postern was an archway in a stretch of the city wall which ran from the castle down to the river. After you'd gone through the arch you'd find cottages which petered out before the lane turned a right-angled bend and made for Castlegate. Here you might get your biggest surprise because Castlegate extended nearly up to the present museum. If you turned down that way you'd pass the four-storey house of the Waud family, said to be very elegantly furnished. Its large garden contained Clifford's Tower which actually belonged to them. The mound was covered in shrubs and they liked to think of it as a romantic ruin. These were the days when Sir Walter Scott was glamorising knights and ruins, although a York Quaker publisher had refused to publish his work because it was 'too worldly'.

8

Castlegate led you to an ancient gateway into the castle precincts and here was a strange anomaly – a castle wall without a castle inside it. Whilst Clifford's Tower was in a private garden, the castle walls enclosed two 'modern' prisons and the law courts with an open space between them where deer browsed and you could see the ravens for all the world as if you were at the Tower of London. The whole area was called the Castle but didn't look much like one. There will be more about that in our later chapter about the prison.

York was a fascinating muddle of contrasts. Medieval jettied houses stood cheek by jowl with tall new homes with broad fenestration. In just the same way poverty and affluence were only a stone's throw from each other. Castlegate was typical. The Fairfax town house (then owned by Peregrine Wentworth and now open to the public and well worth a visit) was expensively appointed and had a riverside garden sloping down to the Foss where Fenwicks now stands. Yet a little farther up Castlegate you came to the first of three mean streets which ran down to the Ouse. These were the famous, or infamous, Water Lanes.

They ran steeply downhill to the river and more or less shared a name since they were unimaginatively known as First Water Lane, Second Water Lane and Far Water Lane. The last of them was on the site of the present Friargate and even managed to be called that before the end of our period. There was no Clifford Street in those days and the three Water Lanes extended from Castlegate all the way to the river. Friargate was the only one of them where there was enough room to drive a carriage – although the coachman needed to be very good at his job because there was only just sufficient space to turn into the street and nowhere in the whole length of it where two vehicles could pass.

Robberies were planned in the Water Lanes which had the worst reputation of any part of York. This was partly because some people lived in desperate poverty, so desperate that they stole to feed their families. If caught, they might be hanged, not that they were very likely to be caught because there was no proper police force. There were over 200 crimes which carried the death penalty, although the inhabitants of Water Lanes couldn't commit some of them (such as cutting down a tree in Downing Street) but they definitely committed others. For them the old adage 'May as well be hung for a sheep as a lamb' meant something. The unfortunate solitary passer-by, who witnessed a burglary, might be murdered to keep him silent; and in such narrow alleys it would be almost impossible to escape a pursuer who probably had accomplices.

However, well-dressed people probably didn't often walk down there. A gentleman with a gold fob watch would risk attack and a lady in long muslin skirts would get her dainty frilled hem lavishly splashed with mud.

Despite its seedy, run-down character, First Water Lane contained some ancient houses of decayed beauty. Wooden brackets under their jetties were carefully carved, their windows and doors were churchlike but these Gothic remnants were rotting away.

Apart from these areas, the pattern of streets within York's walls was much the same as it is today although, without any Victorian or 20th century architecture, the buildings were a mixture of Georgian terraces and medieval gables. Also there was more grass and trees; Toft Green, now the home of the railway offices, was covered by a market garden famous for its trees and shrubs. On each side of Walmgate, behind the houses, were small gardens and open spaces. Traffic to and from Hull used this route.

Passengers for that port could go to the White Swan in Pavement and avail themselves of reduced fares on the True Briton. This coach, which had come from Leeds, left York via Fossgate passing Sunman's shop where one could buy cheap straw hats, and crossing the Foss by the bridge where fearless boys used to walk on the ledge scaring older people who vowed one of them would fall into the river. In 1811 the solid sides of the bridge were removed and an elegant balustrade substituted.

Boys were not the only danger. When William Storrey was driving the Hull coach over that bridge he crushed two pedestrians 'for want of proper attention', as he afterwards admitted, 'by which means they were much injured'. He gave them a written promise to pay all their resultant expenses but had to sign it with a thumb print, being better able to use a whip than a pen. Illiteracy wasn't uncommon since there was no free state education.

In Regency days the Minster (which they usually called the Cathedral) dominated the skyline, accompanied by the spires of city churches but

Stage Coach in Winter.

10

Lop Lane (or Little Blake Street)

unrivalled by anything like a modern office block. However, there is one view of the Minster which is clearer today.

That is the view of the west end. Duncombe Place wasn't there; Lop Lane was and the only building left from it is the Red House which still owns its link-snuffer but has lost the street it stood in. A narrow road it was, too, running from the top of Blake Street to an old arched gateway which opened onto the Cathedral close, a wide space where people could walk around and admire the Gothic magnificence where generations of their ancestors had worshipped.

It was from near here that northbound coaches turned into Bootham and left York through the old bar. That was the best way to go – by coach; on foot was terrible. The ground under the bar was filthy with cattle droppings (and human waste, too) so that the long-skirted ladies were ill-advised to tread there.

On the outside of the bar, cottages hid the wall of St Mary's Abbey and the entrance to Gillygate was narrower than today. Many of Bootham's Georgian houses have survived. The coach passed Marygate and Bootham Row, then the 'Lunatic Asylum', with its frightening reputation for neglect, and a little row of houses (for 10 poor widows) entered by a Norman gateway taken from Holy Trinity, Micklegate. Then the coach

11

thundered through the fields to the village of Clifton with its farming community and there we will leave it because we are getting too far away from York.

Back to the walls now – there wasn't very much outside them. Lord Mayor's Walk was a fashionable promenade but, of course, there was no St John's College beside it. Between Lord Mayor's Walk and Monkgate were the Groves, green land where young men had been drilling to defeat Boney if he landed. There were houses in Monkgate; some of them are still there. Barker Hill led from there to Layerthorpe and a stretch of water called the King's Fishpool, not that George III had ever seen it but under his Norman ancestor the Foss had been dammed to create it. Fishergate hugged the old wall to Castlegate Postern Lane and on the other side of the ferry Baile Hill led to Baggergate Lane, more familiar to us as Nunnery Lane.

Seen from afar York was a brick and timber island in a sea of green land framed by windmills and river water in February 1811 when George, Prince of Wales, took the oath which made him the Regent.

York from Severus Hill.

12

A Look at the People

ON THE WHOLE THE PEOPLE of Regency York presented a straight slim profile because the fashions emphasised the slender and the tall, except where the tight pantaloons and striped waistcoat turned a portly man into a living Toby jug. White muslin tied high under the bust with a modish sash was very unkind to ladies with a fuller figure, too. In fact, the Regency years were a gift to cartoonists such as Rowlandson.

Our city's streets were frequently enlivened with the splash of scarlet as one of the men training to fight Napoleon strode down them. The Redcoats (*Rosbifs* to the French) were nicknamed Salamanca Lobsters after they won that battle in 1812. The poppy-red coat was accompanied by a crimson sash if the man was an officer. Trousers were narrow and white or

Woman wearing yellow silk gown of c.1814.

British Soldier.

13

grey, they were tucked into boots – often Hessians like the civilians wore. The hat was a shako, taller in front and black, adorned with the brass plate which denoted the regiment.

The presence of the cavalry barracks on the site in Fulford used by the army today and the existence of the York City Militia as well as local volunteers must have given York a considerable military presence.

Probably an occasional naval officer, home on leave, may have been seen in his dark blue coat and gold epaulettes, but only if he was on Admiralty business since the Royal Navy didn't like its officers to wear uniforms on shore and non-commissioned men had no official uniform to wear, although they frequently dressed in straw hats, striped jumpers and shapeless trousers. Young officers had already begun to replace the Bobby Shaftoe-style buckled shoes with the fashionable Hessian boots worn by their military and civilian contemporaries.

There must have been hundreds of pairs of Hessians tramping York's streets. They were tall black boots with a jaunty tassel at the front but they were cut a little lower at the back to allow the knee to bend. The leader of London fashion, Beau Brummel, wore his mirror-bright; York gentlemen could get a gloss on theirs by going to Watson, Logan and Coates, the shop which stocked Warren's Original Japan Liquid Blacking for Boots and Shoes. It was sold in stone bottles at one shilling and sixpence a pint. The advertisement described it without modesty: 'This composition produces the most exquisite Jet Black ever beheld . . . It is likewise recommended for Ladies' Half Boots . . . which will experience a brilliancy equal to the highest Japan varnish, be rendered waterproof, and will not soil the clothes.'

The Hessian boots were worn with tight pantaloons of a light shade so it was just as well that the blacking did not soil them. Above these the fashionable man would be sporting a white shirt whose frilled front showed in the V-shape of a waistcoat which finished in a straight line at the waist. His coat was cut away there and had tails at the back. On his short, curled hair he had a hat not unlike the topper but often brown and made of a furred felt called Beaver. Blue was the favourite colour for coats but this might be hidden in cold weather by a buff caped driving coat very like the coachmen wore.

Ladies, too, sometimes wore this buff-coloured cloth which gave us the word 'drab'. It was often used for a pelisse, their version of a winter coat which was a long slim garment and could also be of cotton or silk. In less cold weather this would be replaced by a Spencer which did the duty of a modern cardigan but was more elegant, being a tiny fitted jacket which hugged the bust and stopped short of the natural waist. Regency females wore their gowns with the waistline beneath the breasts which gave a long-line skirt suited to people who were, on average, shorter than we are. In the early years white muslin (sometimes sprigged or spotted) was very commonly used for gowns; patterned cotton was fashionable, too.

The bonnet was the crowning glory. At first small and jockey-shaped, it dictated the hair-style which involved twisting long curls into a chignon and stowing this into the crown. Round about the time of Waterloo a higher crown appeared and then the chignon became a top-knot to fit into this and the face was becomingly framed by a brim. Flowers, ribbons and feathers adorned these millinery masterpieces.

York ladies, reading about London fashions, could follow them without taking the 29½ hour journey to London. They needed only to visit Cooke's shop in Coney Street because, as his advertisement in the *York Herald* stated: 'J.C. begs leave to inform them that he has returned from London, where he purchased a fashionable and an extensive stock of straw and chip hats and bonnets in the greatest variety, and at all prices, also a new stock of trimming ribbons, feathers and flowers, selected from the most fashionable houses in London. The above are now ready for ladies' inspection, whose call will confer a favour . . .' There was also a Mrs Court who sold 'Neat and fashionable straw bonnets'. She, too, begged leave to inform 'the ladies of the vicinity' about her new stock – a rather different approach from the hard-sell telephone calls of today!

The ladies' finery might be protected by umbrellas of gingham or silk sold by a Quaker, William Alexander, who had the bookshop in Castlegate. The upper floors of his premises are still there above Stephenson's Estate Agents and a replica of his shop front may be seen in the Castle Museum. Amongst his paper hangings and writing desks you could also purchase parasols to protect the complexion. But if the parasol didn't do its work properly 'To render more captivating the Charms of Female Beauty', Mrs Vincent's Gowland's Lotion was advertised for sale from Messrs Cattle, W. Spence, T. Deighton and Wolstenholme's.

Ready-to-wear clothes were almost unobtainable. The fashionable lady either made her own gowns or employed a dressmaker.

The slim silhouette was common for day and evening wear but the high neck and long sleeves of the 'morning gown' gave place to a low décolletage with tiny puffed sleeves after dark. Despite war with France, Paris fashions were described in York newspapers. So the young lady living in Micklegate in 1811 read of a Parisian ball dress 'of white crape, ornamented with white satin in a leaf pattern, the bottom of the dress trimmed with pale French roses, and a plaiting of green and root-coloured ribband mixed; short bell sleeves; Persian fringed sash . . .' However was she going to make it?

15

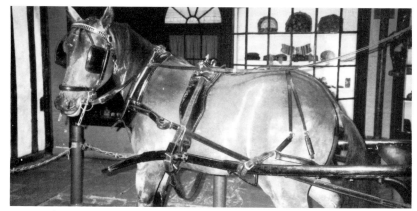

Horse in harness, c.1890. Earlier in the century, Regency ladies might drive to the shops in phaetons.

Not at all, if Papa was willing to pay Steventon and Bownas, the dressmakers in Little Blake Street. The fabric might be obtained from W. Welbank, the linen-draper in Minster Yard. However, if Mama with her English pear-shaped figure wanted something similar, she would need the assistance of Mrs Cooper who advertised: 'Newest patterns of the most approved and fashionable long stays and corsets, from some of the first houses in London, which are most admirable for their fitting and are put on with the greatest facility . . . superior to any for ease and elegance.' Ladies from outside York could send their old stays as a pattern so they could 'be fitted with the greatest exactness and dispatch'.

Older people might be more interested in furs and gloves from Thomas Fowler in Spurriergate and his 'regular assortment of the Patent Fleecy Hosiery for the winter season'.

In fashionable Bootham and Micklegate the ladies in their upstairs drawing rooms wore white caps of thin cotton or spotted muslin adorned with ribbons or frilled, and tied in a bow under the chin. What a disgrace if one were seen without one's cap!

Even women in Water Lane wore caps, sometimes made of unbleached cotton with a small brim to shade the face, rather like a peaked cap. A poor woman had her pride and dressed in the same high-waisted style as her more fortunate contemporaries but often added a kerchief collar such as her mother had worn in the late 18th century. Aprons and shawls were natural additions but sometimes the skirt was hitched up to hold things which also helped to keep it clear of the mud.

Working men usually wore a sleeveless waistcoat over a white shirt plus knee-breeches, stockings and large laced shoes with a slouch hat. A few, probably coming in from the country with market produce, wore smocks. Inevitably certain jobs forced men to dress differently from their friends.

York had a number of blacksmiths who would be very busy in a city filled with horse-drawn transport. The smith wore a fringed leather apron split in the centre so he could draw the horse's leg through the gap and work on the hoof.

The gentleman who brought his riding horse to be shod would be appropriately clad in buckskin breeches with top boots (the sort sometimes exaggerated on stage in pantomimes) which sported light-coloured tops turned down like a cuff. If his wife rode with him, she would use a side-saddle and wear a habit (a long skirt and jacket) which might be made by Hurworth and Son, the tailors in Micklegate.

Many professional men – clergy, doctors and lawyers, still wore the powdered wigs of the 18th century and some older gentlemen wouldn't be seen without one; it was a useful device for covering a bald pate. You could buy a wig or get your hair cut at Parson's in Blake Street which had a large assortment of 'Gentlemen's perukes and ladies' ornamental hair of every description now worn'. False hair pieces could be bought from William Hands opposite the Assembly Rooms but you might not need these if you shopped at Spence's, Wolstenholme's or Deighton's because they sold Macassar oil for the hair described as 'far beyond eulogium for increasing the growth of hair, even on bald places, to a beautiful length and thickness'.

Naturally York streets were not so thronged as they are today but there were plenty of people in them, from the woman who opened Castlegate Postern and the scavenger who collected the rubbish to the Lord Mayor alighting from his coach at the Mansion House. Drovers brought herds of cattle to market; charity children were marched into school.

The bustle and noise didn't all stop when dusk brought the lamplighter with his can of whale oil to fill the parish lamps. Ladies in evening gowns were carried to the Assembly Rooms in sedan chairs and whilst they danced and played cards, the chairmen drank in the basement, insulted each other and brawled noisily. However, if the chairman you employed used abusive language to you or overcharged you, and you had a reliable witness of this, he was fined 10 shillings.

Weddings might draw onlookers but were not such grand occasions as they are now and wedding veils were only just coming into fashion; most brides simply had a new bonnet. However, a funeral could be a really big occasion disrupting the streets in grand style as the hearse was pulled by horses with black plumes on their bridles and followed by as many gentlemen with black hat bands as the family of the deceased could muster; women seldom attended.

17

Travellers, who disliked public coaches and could afford to hire a conveyance, might enter York in a post-chaise. This carriage had just one fixed seat which could accommodate three people, if they weren't too large! They sat facing the horses and were driven by a postillion whose livery was chosen by the inn which owned the vehicle. Often coats and carriages were yellow, giving the equipage the nickname 'Yellow Bounder'.

Children were often dressed like miniature adults, so a boy wore a tailed coat but his trousers were not so tightly fitting as his father's pantaloons. Little girls could easily run and play in their high-waisted cotton dresses; some of them wore the new fashion of pantalettes – long white drawers with a lacy frill near the ankles which showed below the skirt. Not many of their mothers wore these, although some wore drawers but wouldn't admit it because drawers were thought by many to be an immoral garment for a grown woman.

Nightcaps were worn in bed by both men and women – a tasselled one for the husband, a small bonnet-style tied under the chin for his wife.

Outside the Watch (or the Charley as many people called him) tramped up and down, calling the hours and the weather. In slouch hat and greatcoat with huge shoes, he carried a staff, lantern and rattle with which he could try to summon help. He was supposed to apprehend housebreakers, if he saw them, but only in his own parish. Neither gales nor snow kept him from the streets but each Charley had a refuge which looked rather like a sentry box; one of them may be seen today in the Castle Museum.

In the costume gallery of this museum are two Regency dresses showing us the Belle of the evening with a fashionable stole, which she would have called a scarf, draped over her arms and a dainty fan for flirting or cooling according to her mood.

It is difficult to believe that she lived in the same city as the chimney sweep's ragged apprentice or the coal heaver unloading a Humber keel at the wharf in Marygate. York was a city of contrasts indeed.

Old Watchman

18

Fire! Fire!

WHEN PARLIAMENT DECIDED THAT THE powers of the ailing George III should be devolved on his son, naturally people didn't say, 'We'll pull down our houses, build new homes in the Grecian style and call them Regency'. Most people continued living at the houses built earlier in the King's reign and that of his grandfather. These typical Georgian houses may still be seen in many of York's streets.

They were usually built of brick with stone facings and a fanlight over the door admitting light to the narrow hall. At the side of the front door was an iron or copper object like an inverted ice cream cone; this was the link-snuffer. Nervous persons, out in darkness, could hire a boy who walked beside them carrying his 'link' – a naked flame which resembled the Olympic torch. When he had seen you safely to your home, he stuffed the torch into your link-snuffer which extinguished the light. These links were just one of the fire hazards in Regency York.

Link Snuffer   *Fire Mark*

19

*The Garforths'
Town House with
area in Micklegate.*

There were other hazards, too. The kitchen was in the basement; its door opened into a small yard called the 'area' to which there was outside access for tradesmen and servants down a flight of stone steps. People walking along the dimly-lit pavement would have fallen into the area if the home owner hadn't installed iron railings as a safeguard.

Kitchen maids often slept in the attics four or five storeys above their subterranean kitchen where the *'batterie de cuisine'* (a set of copper pans and jelly moulds) gleamed in the firelight. Meat was roasted on a spit, almost barbecuelike and its fat spurtled down into a dripping pan; bread and pies were baked in an oven beside the fire.

Hot cinders from this were put in a copper warming pan and taken upstairs to heat the sheets of four-poster beds. Every room had its fireplace, so necessary when the potentials of gas and electricity hadn't been explored.

There were candles everywhere, mounted in crystal chandeliers, for those who could afford them, sending sparkling light from the glass droplets. Branches of candles were placed strategically beside mirrors so the reflection gave added brightness. The drawing rooms of Micklegate's larger houses could be as bright as electricity makes ours today; but the domestic staff, sleeping under the eaves or scrubbing below stairs, used tallow candles which they made of mutton fat (a smelly job!) which gave a yellow light but cost far less than the beeswax candles used by county families like the Bourchiers who had a country estate and a town house in York.

In Water Lane they'd often make do with rushlights. Rushes would be collected near the Ouse and dipped in fat to make a thin candle which was put in an iron holder made by the blacksmith. It was lit with a taper from the fire or you could use a tinder box.

It's easy to see what an inflammable place York was, especially when we remember that a large proportion of its buildings were timber-framed remnants of Tudor and medieval times. Small wonder that the prudent householder subscribed to one of the insurance companies!

And they probably wouldn't have made much profit if each hadn't kept its own fire brigade to put out the flames before they destroyed all that was insured. The householder was given a plaque to display on his home showing which company insured his property. At first these were made of lead and had the policy number on them; later they were copper without the number but embossed with the sign of the company on them. The Royal Exchange (whose York agent was Mr Richard Townend) used a picture of the London Exchange building with a crown over it. Many local people insured with the Sun and its copper mark was like a child's drawing of a round sun with a face and rays protruding from it. There are examples of this still to be seen on some houses in Bootham.

The Yorkshire County Fire Office had an impressive list of trustees headed by the Duke of Rutland, the Marquis of Buckingham and the Earls of Northampton, Buckinghamshire and Upper Ossory. This company declared that its benefits encouraged the Directors 'to make it as extensively useful as possible, and induce them again to submit its principles to a discerning public'. However, the discerning public might decide to insure with the British Fire Office whose York agents were W. Blanchard and Son and whose mark was a *lion passant* in a decorative circle. The average rate of insurance with them was two shillings per cent per annum but if your property was 'hazardous' you paid three shillings and 'doubly hazardous' cost you five shillings which you paid if the property was constructed of a lot of wood or if 'the nature of the trade or manufacture' made fire more likely. It's to be hoped that Mr Whincup of Walmgate had paid the doubly hazardous rate because his shelling mill caught fire on the 2nd of November in 1813 and not only burnt down but destroyed a large amount of corn stored there. Three thousand pounds worth of damage he suffered, enough money to keep several families for several years.

One company offering fire insurance was named appropriately 'Phoenix' and its mark showed the mythological bird rising from the ashes. This would also appear on its leather fire buckets.

Each parish was legally forced to keep a fire engine and usually had long fire hooks, too, which were poles with double iron hooks on the end to pull blazing thatch or anything else movable away from the conflagration. But it wasn't a good idea to depend on the parish fire engine since the local parish officers tended to employ elderly people to man it and, despite the best intentions, they weren't exactly efficient amidst choking smoke and crackling timbers.

Anyway, all the fire engines were very limited in their dousing capacity. A couple of them can still be seen in the Castle Museum. Made of wood with iron-rimmed wheels, they were horse-drawn and had a lead-lined tank to hold the water and a copper pipe to direct it onto the burning building.

'Victoria', one of the late Eighteenth Century Fire Engines in York Castle Museum.

If your house caught fire, you would soon have a crowd of sightseers, some of them glad of excitement and others anxious lest the blaze spread to their own homes. A message would be sent rapidly to the insurance company but there was a little time before you could expect the engine, so strenuous efforts had to be made. Burning fat in the kitchen might be smothered but, if someone had fallen asleep with their bedside candle still burning, the bed curtains were probably on fire and half the room with them. The clattering hooves and rumbling wheels of the approaching engine would be a relief.

Even then the firemen might look at the copper plaque on the house to make sure you were really insured with them! Bystanders would be pressed into service to work the horizontal wooden bars which turned the iron axle and pumped water from the tank into the copper pipe. It must have been warm work added to the sense of urgency and the heat from the burning house. The tank didn't hold enough water for your needs and people would run with buckets to the parish pump or the river if that was nearer.

It wasn't wise to get too near the damaged house; a few months after the death of George III, a building was destroyed by fire in North Street and the subsequent day one of the blackened walls collapsed, killing a boy and girl.

The strength and direction of the wind could make all the difference to fire-fighters but, if the fire wasn't extinguished early on, it was unlikely that you could do more than prevent it spreading down the street. People were very apprehensive of fires, although this didn't stop them having a firework display when a circus was held outside Bootham. Yet there must have been some nervous head-shaking when the *York Chronicle* reported in October 1811 on a fire in Cambridge where a gentleman was awakened at night 'by the crackling of the fire which raged with such excessive fury that he was considerably scorched before he could make his escape'. After a detailed description of the fire-fighting, the *Chronicle* concluded, 'We have the consolation to add that no lives were lost on this lamentable and distressing occasion'.

Fire Buckets made of wood and leather, Nineteenth Century.

23

A Pretty Kettle of Fish

THE MAIN DIFFERENCE BETWEEN OUR eating habits and those of Regency people in York was their total lack of convenience foods. In the absence of plastic, foil and Government health warnings, they ate whatever fresh food was available.

Not that it was always perfectly fresh. Some strange things happened to milk between the cow and the kitchen.

Bread, cheese and weak beer was probably the staple diet of Water Lane, as it was of most poor people.

The privileged inhabitants of Bootham and Micklegate would wake (not too early) to a light breakfast of the tea and toast variety – although it might be chocolate, if they were old-fashioned; even coffee started the day for some. It could make its appearance in an elegant pot of the local creamware manufactured in Leeds. Some folk preferred wiggs to toast and this type of bread was a reminder of the bald head surmounted by a wig still popular with grandfathers and lawyers, for it got its name from its resemblance to a wig resting overnight on a wooden wig-stand, the bread bun being topped by a cheese sauce. You could have your wiggs plain with marmalade made from Seville oranges but you would be unlikely to have what we commonly think of as a traditional English breakfast of eggs and bacon. Gentlemen with hearty appetites were perfectly capable of consuming roast beef but the majority would leave such feasting for dinner (five o'clock for very old-fashioned persons and seven for those who liked to think they behaved like Mayfair aristocrats).

Cold meat might make an appearance with fruit in the middle of the day for a 'nuncheon', not to be confused with the three-course luncheon which hadn't yet become the mode.

Soup and fish made their début early at dinner because the empty dishes would look messy and so were removed after use to leave the table covered with a variety of provender arranged with an eye for colour and detail. There would be more than one main meat dish in the central part of the table such as Hunter's Beef where 'To a round of beef that weighs twenty-five pounds' you should 'take three ounces of saltpetre, three ounces of the coarsest sugar, an ounce of cloves and three handfuls of common salt . . .' This had to hang for two or three days before use and

*Eighteenth Century
dining room at
York Castle Museum.*

probably only some of it was brought to the table to take its place with a 'Green Goose' or perhaps 'Shoulder of Lamb Forced with Sorrel Sauce'. The point was that you wanted to put your main dishes in the centre and add the 'Pretty side dishes' for their colourful appearance such as a 'Jelly of Pigs Feet and Ears' which was put to set in a mould shaped like a melon. Vegetables were regarded as rather plebeian but could be placed on the table for the introduction of a little more colour, for example the peas arranged in a lettuce leaf, which we know that the Fairfaxes included on their table in Castlegate. The exhibition set up at Fairfax House in 1990 showed beautifully the artistry of York's cooks when it came to making a banquet look luscious.

The second course was similarly arranged to the first but contained sweet foods as well as savoury. No one was expected to partake of every dish but unfortunately on formal occasions you didn't get a choice from the full range as it was considered polite to sample only the dishes near you, so you might look longingly at the Fricassee of Veal whilst being obliged to eat from the White Hog's Puddings.

One thing you needn't do was starve, for when the 20 or so dishes had been removed and the cloth taken away, the sweetmeats arrived and a very attractive set they were. If the cook had studied *The Experienced English Housekeeper, For The Use of Ladies, Housekeepers, Cooks, &c. Written purely from Practice* by Elizabeth Raffald, she would be able to spin sugar like a silver web. If she bought from William Alexander's bookshop a copy of *A New System of Domestic Cookery; Formed upon Principles of Economy; and adapted to the use of Private Families, By A Lady,* she would find how to make Puits d'Amour and Floating Islands to enhance the table.

When the ladies rose, the gentlemen got down to the serious business of the evening – damning the French and toasting Wellington in their host's best port. It was some time before they joined their gossiping wives in the drawing room for cards or music. This involved some young women suffering agonies of embarrassment or the delights of showing off (according to character) by singing ballads for the soporific company.

Then, in case anyone was feeling peckish, they served a light supper of cold meat, fruits and sweets at the very least but, if the hostess was jealous of her reputation, one or two hot dishes, too.

It is to be hoped they did not forget the tattered inhabitants of the Bedern and Water Lanes. Probably they didn't. The Lady who wrote *Domestic Cookery* evidently expected her readers to think of them for she devoted a chapter to 'Cookery for the Poor'. Her recommendations included this advice: 'Cut a very thick upper crust of bread, and put it into the pot where salt beef is boiling and near ready; it will attract some of the fat, and when swelled out, will be no unpalatable dish to those who rarely taste meat.'

The smell of meat would often have permeated the basement kitchens of York, more than the crusty smell of bread because that was not usually baked at home as there were enough bakeries to supply most of the wants of Regency York. In Spurriergate J. Elliott, the confectioner and pastry-cook, did not hesitate to describe his wares as 'Epicurean Perfection' although as there was no Trades Description Act we don't know how truthful he was. He certainly provided for the imperfections of home cooks for they could buy sauces from him, such as 'Oyster Catsup' which may not strike us as a very attractive way of naming a sauce but the ketchup of today seems to be derived from the Catsups of a previous era. Walnut Ketchup was sometimes made at home but in 1812 the 'most admired Fish Sauce now extant is Purkis's Essence of Lobsters (newly invented)' and Mr Elliott sold that, too.

Old Thursday Market Cross.

When cooks wanted to provide a suitable fish dish for use under the Essence of Lobsters, they went to one of the markets for their purchase. Neither of these was on the site of the present market. Freshwater fish could be bought in the Thursday Market, which was also open on Saturdays and situated in the present St Sampson's Square. Many kinds of river fish were popular; the cook might want carp, tench and gudgeon or she might be going to make 'Eel Broth', recommended for its nourishing quality. If she was shopping before 1815, she might have eyed the market hall rather warily as it had become the haunt of 'dissolute persons' which is why it was demolished in the year of Waterloo.

Enterprising cooks might deplore their inability to get sturgeon but the Lady who wrote *Domestic Cookery* told her readers how to make 'an excellent imitation of pickled sturgeon'. For this you had to 'take a fine large turkey, but not old; pick it very nicely, singe, and make it extremely clean: bone and wash it, and tie it across and across with a bit of mat-string washed clean'. After boiling it, you put a two pound weight on it and then pickled it, after which it was to be served with fennel.

Sea fish could be obtained at the market in Pavement. Its market cross was pulled down in 1813 but not apparently for the same interesting

27

reason as the hall in the Thursday Market; in the Pavement, where corn was sold, there simply wasn't enough room for all the stalls so the cross went and the buyers and sellers, who had sheltered under its circular roof supported by pillars, shivered and got wet in the interests of more trade.

Fish might be fried in a thick-bottomed pan on the fire but most kitchens would possess at least one 'fish kettle', which was a part of the *batterie de cuisine*. Made of copper but lined with tin, it was shaped like the fish it was meant to hold.

If we were able to look into a Regency kitchen (and there's an 18th century one in Fairfax House) we should be most conscious of the glowing fire and gleaming copper. Blue and white china would line the shelves of the dresser; game and ham would be suspended from ceiling hooks and the great scrubbed table might support a huge cheese and a large conical sugar loaf. A skillet, which was a pan with feet like the one in the Castle Museum, would be keeping a sauce warm beside the range.

Yet we should recognise many utensils such as the pastry cutters and rolling pin which haven't changed much.

A lot of food was the same, too; beef, lamb, mutton, chicken, fresh vegetables and dairy products were as familiar to our Regency ancestors as they are to us. Nor was everything homemade, for example you could buy brawn at the confectioner's in Coney Street. You could even get food from abroad. Sugar beet was rare and most of our sugar came from the West Indies; molasses and rum were brought across the Atlantic in convoys of merchant ships escorted by frigates of the Royal Navy to keep them safe from French attack. Oranges filled up the spaces in cargo ships which carried wine from our ally Portugal. Many goods were trans-shipped at Hull and reached York up the Ouse.

There was plenty of choice at the grocer's and one of the most reputable grocers was Tukes in Castlegate, the 'ancestor' of Rowntrees. The Tukes were a Quaker family with a strong social conscience; William Tuke started The Retreat, one of the first institutions to treat mental illness with compassion.

A butter market beside the church of St Martin-cum-Gregory in Micklegate, supplied the wholesale requirements of all north-eastern England. The corn market in Pavement began with the ringing of a church bell at eleven in the morning. Cooks could buy many different foods there.

In *Domestic Cookery* the 'Lady' gave advice on how to choose fresh meat. 'Ox-beef is the richest and largest, but in small families, and to some tastes, heifer-beef is better if finely fed.'

Meat and vegetables might be boiled in a cauldron suspended from a 'crane' in the kitchen chimney. There was also a similar arrangement

The Dessert Course at Fairfax House.

which allowed you to tip the heavy copper kettle without taking it off the hook; this was called an 'idle-back'. The water needed boiling for it came usually from a well, although some people subscribed to the waterworks and received piped water three days a week.

There was plenty to satisfy those with a sweet tooth – syllabub, 'genteel pudding', ratafia cream and other delights. After that it might be necessary to buy Butler's Restorative Tooth Powder, available in York from Dancer, Champlay and James. Its advertisement stated: 'Beautiful white teeth may be regarded as one of the greatest blessings Providence can bestow, without which the finest formed face is imperfect . . . Butler's Restorative Tooth Powder is a most elegant and certain remedy for all diseases of the teeth and gums; its particular qualities are not simply confined to cleansing the teeth, but will preserve them in the highest state of perfection; it will render them beautifully white, fasten such as may be loose, and restore them to their original purity . . .'

Perhaps people bought it in the hope that it might save them from a visit to Messrs Horner and Turner, the appropriately named dentists in Coney Street.

Twopence Coloured

IN REGENCY TIMES PEOPLE GOT up early and worked hard – most of them, but there was entertainment for those who could afford it. The Theatre Royal was on its present site but hidden from view. St Leonard's Place didn't exist and the grounds of the medieval St Leonard's Hospital covered most of that area. The only way into the theatre was from Lop Lane (the present Duncombe Place). The entrance was sandwiched between Red House and the next house but it was roofed so people arriving in sedan chairs could alight under cover. They then had to negotiate a narrow passage shaped like a dog's hind leg; everyone jostled together, ladies in French fashions whose escorts had paid for a box and the *hoi polloi* who had spent a shilling to get a place in the Upper Gallery.

When they reached the theatre, they entered a square auditorium with galleries resting on oak pillars and a row of boxes on each side culminating with those over the stage doors. It was brightly lit with wax candles in brass chandeliers and in the footlights. However, this had its disadvantages because the lights couldn't be dimmed during the performance. On the other hand, if the play bored you, it was easy to look round and see who was there and what they were wearing. Not that everyone was polite and quiet when bored, and being able to gaze at the rest of the audience wasn't recompense enough for some of those in the pit who complained that hot wax dripped onto their heads. Urgent voices would interrupt the scene by calling: 'Snuffer!' to the man employed to attend to those guttering candles. Bald·gentlemen probably longed for the wigs their fathers had worn. However, in 1818 new chandeliers were installed which were shaped to collect the drips. Comfort was important, for the evening's entertainment usually lasted five hours at least.

The scenery was quite realistic, landscapes well-painted and rooms made in a correct box shape. Costumes had improved and if the play was set in a previous age, some attempt was made to produce accurate historic costumes – a new venture which must have been pleasing to those who had once watched Romeo in knee breeches and a lace jabot. But Regency people did not leave Romeo alone for they produced a happy ending to the play sometimes. Shakespeare was not sacrosanct. The costumes and scenery were said to be spectacular in September 1812 when Mrs McGibbon took the part of the Princess of Mingrelia in *The Dramatic Romance of Timor the Tartar*.

The Red House and Tate Wilkinson's Home.

In July 1811 the public were 'most respectfully informed that Mrs Jordan is engaged for six nights and will make her appearance on Thursday, August 1, in her celebrated character of *The Country Girl*'. A box at the theatre cost four shillings, a seat downstairs was 2s 6d. However, it might be worthwhile to endure the discomfort of the Upper Gallery (price one shilling) for Mrs Jordan had already stunned London in this rôle. She was a dark-eyed young woman who loved life and charmed the audience – not only the audience; she bore 10 children to a Royal Duke. She remained the mistress of the Duke of Clarence until 1816, but it was on a previous visit to York that she had first taken the title of Mrs Jordan to add a touch of respectability to her popularity. It was also in York that she got nicknamed Mrs Wilfull for her temperamental outbursts.

If it wasn't worth a shilling to see the Royal concubine, at least you were promised after the play a song by Mr Russell and the 'favourite farce of Raising the Wind'. Not bad for 12 pence, seeing that *The Country Girl* ran to five acts. The actors and actresses were always advertised formally with the title of Mr, Mrs, or Miss and the company were known as His

Majesty's Servants of the Theatre Royal, York, a title bestowed on them by Act of Parliament. The regular performers were locally popular and, if the theatre-going public wanted a permanent reminder of a well-known actor, they could buy a printed drawing of him or her, penny plain or twopence coloured.

The evening's entertainment was usually made up of two plays (one serious and one farce) and one or more songs. Most of the singing was done by Miss Horribow and Miss Rennell but there were male soloists as, for instance, when *Mother Goose* was first performed here and Mr Hall sang a piece called *Push Along* and Mr Bailey followed with a comic song. One doesn't know if he was also singing a comic song in July 1815 when his solo was entitled *The Duke of Wellington the Dandy*; possibly so, for the Duke was already known as The Beau by his soldiers – those of them who didn't call him 'Old Nosey'. Mr Want was certainly *not* singing a comic song when he rendered *The Death of Nelson,* for it was only 10 years since England's favourite hero was killed at Trafalgar.

There was a new programme nearly every day of a six-day week. Sometimes an old favourite from the repertoire was performed again but probably accompanied by a new play as well. If people chose to watch only one, they could come late or leave early. In Assize week the judge and sheriff might make a request for a particular play. In July 1812 whilst prisoners were arraigned in the Law Courts, Miss Smith appeared at the Theatre Royal in *The Tragedy of Isabella* or *The Fatal Marriage.* There were two seasons for the theatre, one in winter and the other when the Assizes took place and then the Races were on as well. Yorkshire's aristocratic families then left their country estates and came to their town houses in York such as Micklegate House and Castlegate House.

Box office returns were important then as now and special effects might draw custom, for audiences liked something visually satisfying rather than intellectually stimulating, so new inventions were employed. On a March Wednesday in 1815 when *The Woodman's Hut* was performed, the audience was promised that 'The wall of the cottage is struck by lightning and falls, the river is seen through the opening', and 'The piece concludes with the Burning of the Forest, Woodman's Hut, Bridge and Falling of Trees'. Less worrying for the insurance company was the historical drama where Act One showed 'An engagement between a Christian ship and a Barbary Corsair, with the Rising and Bursting of a Water Spout'.

Perhaps young people preferred the performance in 1814 which included the descent of a hot air balloon with three passengers in the 'car' which was a boat-shaped carrier in lieu of a basket. On the other hand they might have been more thrilled on Saturday, August 13, 1814 when, according to the programme, 'Preceding the Play, the Antipodean Powers of the Surprising *Sieur Sanches* will be exercised in the most surprising manner. He will WALK against the CEILING over the stage WITH HIS HEAD DOWNWARDS,' with a flag in each hand and 'at the extremity of his walk will suspend one Leg, turn on his Heel, and walk back.'

This was not the total of Sieur Sanche's talents. He was back on the ceiling again on August 16 when he was billed to 'balance six boys on the slack rope suspended by the heels, in full swing, on his hands, feet and body'. These unfortunates were not the only ones to share in his act. The next night, following the play and a comic opera, he undertook to 'balance Four Heavy Coach Wheels with several Persons on them, while suspended with his Head downwards and the Rope in full Swing!!!'

Did that cause everyone to rush to the Box Office? It was open daily at the theatre from 11 a.m. to 2 p.m. Performances started at seven in the evening but the doors opened at six.

When the Regency began, the theatre was still managed by John Tate Wilkinson, son of the most famous manager; in 1814 it was taken over by Robert Mansell who was succeeded by Fitzgerald in 1818. During the time of John Tate Wilkinson the wardrobe master was Johnny Winter, a colourful Yorkshire character who had very little respect for such new-fangled notions as historic costumes. He said, 'That John Kemble and Shakespeare have given me more trouble than all the other people in the world put together, and my spouse into t'bargain.'

It didn't please Johnny Winter when extra scenic effects were produced but audiences loved them. On Robert Mansell's benefit night in April 1815 the company gave 'A New Melodramatic Play with entirely new Scenery, Machinery, and Decorations, called the *Child of the Desert*'. Most of the actors were given a benefit performance and on this occasion the programme promised splendid scenery including the Square in Baghdad, the 'Turkish burying ground with the Tomb of Ali', and the 'Grand Bridge in the Seraglio Gardens'. At the end of all that Mr Want sang again the *Death of Nelson* and then everyone sat back to enjoy a new musical piece.

Unfortunately there was no amplifying equipment in those days with the result that actors were sometimes obliged to speak in a louder and harsher voice than was appropriate to the words, but they would not be allowed to get away with anything which the audience didn't like. It wasn't worthwhile enduring five hours on a hard bench for substandard acting and benches were the usual seats in a Regency theatre. But the acting would certainly not be substandard when the famous Edmund Kean played at the Theatre Royal in 1819 and it was a tribute to the reputation of York's playhouse that famous stars from London could always be induced to act here in Race Week.

VII

Having Fun Regency-Style

ENTERTAINMENT CENTRED ON ANYTHING WHICH could produce wagers and bets. York's biggest worry when the Regency began was that the new government of the Prince Regent might abolish lotteries and people might lose their slim chances of making a fortune. This was a rather strange fear seeing that the Prince Regent had already lost far more money at dice and cards than most folk would ever see. Anyway, a few weeks after he took the oath as Regent there were sweepstakes of 20 guineas for horses taking part in the first day of the Spring meeting at the Racecourse on the Knavesmire. Mr Rhodes in York and Messrs Weatherby in London and Newmarket were taking the bets. Other sweepstakes, some for as much as 50 guineas, followed.

The races were the highlight of York's fashionable season. Gentlemen and peers from nearby stately homes left their estates for their town houses in York when the races took place. It was they who had originally paid most of the cost of the Grandstand designed by the famous local architect, John Carr. It gave them a good view over the Knavesmire because it had a long upstairs room with a balcony. Some of the elegant arched windows can still be seen although a modern complex has changed the site. On the ground floor the élite could buy refreshments, and anyone wanting lists of horses running and details about the weights they were carrying obtained those from old women handing out this vital information on the course.

York newspapers frequently advertised racehorses for sale; also descriptions of mounts which had been stolen – a daring crime which was punishable by death. This was brought gruesomely to mind on the racecourse by the view of the 'Three-legged Mare', namely the tyburn nearly opposite to the present Pulleyn Drive where hangings took place until the New Drop was used. Finally the Three-legged Mare was taken down in 1812.

The fashionable throng could get evening entertainment as well. The Assembly Rooms (sometimes called the Burlington Rooms after their famous architect) in Blake Street became the mecca for the county visitors in Race Week and at other times. We can still see its large hall which contains 48 Corinthian pillars making a very classical contrast to the small timbered dwellings then lining nearby streets. Lord Burlington had planned a treat for the local inhabitants if Royalty ever condescended to

34

Corinthian Capitals in the Assembly Rooms.

visit his Assembly Rooms; he had placed small windows high above the dance floor with the idea of allowing the curious to climb many feet up on the outside and peer through this bird's eye view at the exalted personages dancing below.

Country dances were the most popular; young men and their partners circled and formed straight lines in organised sets. The couple at the head often 'called the dance' and some dances had a distinctly Yorkshire flavour such as the York Maggot and Tristram Shandy. The quadrille and cotillion were favourites even though partners were kept at arm's length from each other and there wasn't much more excitement than holding hands. However, the waltz had come to England from the Continent and daring young ladies learnt its steps from York dancing masters – to the horror of some older people, one of whom wrote to the *York Chronicle* to express his grave misgivings:

Sirs,

I beg leave . . . to invite the attention of the Parents and Guardians of British female innocence to a new fashion which is just raising its impure head amongst us. I mean the . . . waltz dance, a dance of lewd and licentious nature, imported from those stews of contamination on the Continent . . . If we wish to preserve untainted, that diffidence of character, and modesty of mein [*sic*] and conduct, which so peculiarly grace and distinguish the daughters of Britain above every other nation in Europe, it behoves every parent to shut his door against this foreign underminer of the morals and chastity of his daughter. This harlot dance . . . can only be cultivated here to the pollution and overthrow of those virtues which form the safeguard of British female innocence, and wherein is to be found the best security for the happiness of those who may be united with it in wedlock . . .

Nevertheless fashionable York continued to dance but there were more country dances than waltzes. Even these might prove useful introductions and the Assembly Rooms were something of a marriage bureau. There were many hopeful and excited young ladies who arrived there by carriage, hackney or sedan chair and a lot of older ones, too, who came to watch and gossip. It cost sixpence for half a mile in a sedan chair before ten in the evening and most of the citizens wouldn't have farther than that to go; after ten you paid a shilling but if you wanted to stop and have a word with a friend, the chairmen couldn't charge you more unless you kept them waiting more than 10 minutes. Once the hopeful dancer had been set down in the portico of the Assembly Rooms, the chairmen repaired into the basement where they played dice and cards – possibly winning or losing far more than the fare they had earned that evening. This led to some bloody noses below stairs.

There were cards above stairs, too. Every Monday there were 'Card Assemblies' when the doors of the Assembly Rooms opened at 7 p.m. and there was accompanying music until one in the morning. Mr Haden, the hatter in Coney Street, collected subscriptions for these card assemblies. If you paid 10 shillings and sixpence for the season, it would only cost you one and sixpence to go to an individual card assembly; non-subscribers paid four shillings an evening. The card players enjoyed these entertainments throughout the winter.

Some of them preferred to escape from the whirling butterflies of the ballroom into the Round Room, even on dancing nights because gambling was more exciting than watching the youngsters performing Slingsby's Reel. Hazard or Faro or Deep Basset was far more enthralling; besides, the Round Room was opposite to the Refreshment Room, always a judicious place to be. However, it couldn't rival the grand ballroom for magnificence; there weren't many public rooms in Europe at the time which could do that. Candles glittered in the crystal chandeliers, especially the centre one given by Lord Burlington himself. It was wise to keep a wary eye on the floor for spots of candle grease or the most elegant dance steps could turn into a slide. It got hot with so many people, sometimes 400 or more, and there was hardly any need for the great fireplace which Lord Burlington had donated, a cast-off from his home. There must have been many flushed faces to go out into the frosty night air and the chairmen probably came up the subway from their warm quarters with some reluctance.

PARIS DRESS.

A chair was a 'must' though for the lady who stepped onto that cold road in a full ball gown like the 'Roman robe of pink crape, worn over white gossamer satin', for she was unlikely to feel much warmth from her 'occasional scarf of Paris net, starred with silver' and her white satin slippers ornamented with pink rosettes wouldn't be much protection from dirt in the streets, although no doubt it was comforting to know that Parliament forbade York's citizens to slaughter cattle in the open street or 'throw any dirt into any public drain'.

Special assemblies were held to celebrate important occasions; and the more important occasions that arose the better. Queen Charlotte obligingly had her 68th birthday in February 1812. What better excuse for an entertainment? 'There will be a ball on Friday evening, the 17th instant in honour of the Queen's birthday, on the 18th. The rooms to be opened at eight o'clock.' So ran the advertisement in the newspaper.

But dancing and gaming were not the only attractions and some of them were not as civilised. The cruel practice of cock-fighting was popular enough for there to be several venues for it and the most celebrated was in Bootham, almost opposite to the gates of Bootham Hospital. Birds, fed on barley soaked in sherry and accoutred with wicked spurs, fought courageously while men bet on the results of the 'main' or bout. York possessed its own pack of foxhounds and a circus made visits to the city.

In 1814 the public had the opportunity to see 'a great number of the most astonishing deceptions'. Not a unique experience perhaps for any era but these emanated from Mr Hunt the 'Conjuror', who promised to perform every evening for a week, and announced with satisfaction that he had previously received 'very liberal patronage' from the ladies and gentlemen of York and its vicinity.

For the star-gazers there were lectures illustrated by the 'Dioastrodoxon, or Grand Transparent Orrery', which 'gives the most perspicuous and comprehensive view' of eclipses, comets and almost anything else you cared to name; it was guaranteed to 'charm the Eye, elevate the Mind, and connect the natural with the moral Sense, on a scale of Magnitude and Splendour never yet exhibited in this City'. And to this intellectual feast was added 'The Dulcet Notes of the Celestina'. If you wanted to go, you paid your money to William Spence the bookseller in the Pavement.

It sounds rather more exciting than Mr Matthew's 'Specimens of Ventriloquy' but if you wanted a ticket for that you got it from Mr Knapton's music shop in Coney Street. York people were accustomed to use someone's name and the description of their premises as an address because it had not yet become obligatory to have houses numbered, although the City had been compelled to follow the London method of putting the name on the corner of each street.

York enjoyed the opportunity to see the beginning of one of London's most famous attractions. Madame Tussaud put on her travelling exhibition in Goodramgate where it could be viewed from ten in the morning until 11 p.m. for an entrance fee of a shilling, children allowed in at half price. For this modest amount you could see 'The Grand European Cabinet of Figures Consisting of sixty-nine public characters modelled from life'. Less gruesome than some of her exhibits which had been modelled from death. The poor lady was a refugee from Revolutionary France, whose remarkable talent for modelling in wax had caused the Revolutionary leaders to force her to make wax models of the more famous heads which were severed by the guillotine blade. A devotee of Marie Antoinette, she had nonetheless been compelled to model that Queen's head after her execution. After escaping with her son to England, she had toured the country putting on exhibitions of wax figures to earn a living.

Other entertainments visited York in their tours. In September 1811 there was a circus just outside Bootham which included, besides tightrope dancing, a 'Cotillion with Six Horses'. No wonder that the *York Chronicle* printed a satirical verse by the contemporary playwright, Richard Brinsley Sheridan (then living in Savile Row, Mayfair); lines which were sent to the *Chronicle* by the gentleman who so abhorred the waltz.

> How arts improve in this degenerate age!
> Peers mount the Box, and horses tread the stage;
> While Waltzing Females, with unblushing face,
> Disdain to dance – but in a man's embrace;
> How arts improve, when modesty is dead,
> And taste and sense are like our Bullion fled!

Probably some of York's conventional gentlemen were more shocked by members of the House of Lords driving coaches (the latest craze) than they were by the drain on our finances of war with France, the country which they persisted in blaming for everything from waltzing to eating frogs.

39

Electing the Honourable Member

YORK WAS STILL DISCUSSING THE appearance of a comet and William Herschel was making his observations of it known to the Royal Society when a cataclysmic shock ran through Britain causing *frissons* of horror in York; the impossible had happened, a British Prime Minister had been assassinated. At about five o'clock on the afternoon of May 11, 1812, Spencer Perceval was walking through the lobby of the House, of Commons when he was shot through the heart.

A wave of sympathy for his widow and 12 children induced York's press to print some verses of less than Shakespearean quality:

> With deepest gloom see every brow o'ercast,
> Each visage sunk, and every eye aghast!
> Hark! piteous sounds! the universal groan
> Rever'brates from the cottage to the throne

and 40 more lines to the same effect!

Lord Liverpool was appointed to succeed Perceval and a General Election took place in October.

General Elections were popular because they livened everything up and people, who never had a real holiday, got entertainment and free drinks. Of course, not everybody got a vote but they got plenty of fun. The country was not divided into equal constituencies; the whole county of Yorkshire was represented by two members and voters had to come to York itself to register their votes. No women had the franchise and the only men to do so were those who held property to the value of two pounds a year; they were called the Forty-Shilling Freeholders.

When a contest took place, these fortunate individuals were wined, dined and bribed. Some of them, less lucky, were threatened with what we should call a mugging on their way home if they cast their vote for the 'wrong' candidate. Since there was no ballot, these threats too often came true. The actual voting took place in the space between the prisons and Law Courts now called the Eye of York. Here the Forty-Shilling Freeholder mounted a platform and spoke his choice aloud so it was recorded and his candidate's agent would come later to reimburse him for his expenses in travelling to the county town. If he lived in a remote village, this probably included several nights in inns, where he ate lavishly at the candidate's expense, and some long hours in a stage coach. Not surprisingly it cost a lot to get a seat in Parliament. In 1807 between them the three candidates had spent nearly a quarter of a million pounds, a sum of incredible size in a country where an agricultural labourer might earn not much more than £1 a week.

In October 1812 there were once again three candidates for the two Yorkshire seats and the inns of the city were no doubt hoping to make a lot of money. For those who liked the excitement which results in a few bloody noses the forthcoming election would be full of opportunity. At the previous election a wag had noted this in typical Georgian humour:

> Two voters, by zeal for the candidate led
> Press'd down by the mob, at the Hustings lay dead.
> What a loss to their friends when their fate shall be told!
> 'Not at all', cried an agent – 'They'd both of them poll'd.'

It is only fair to the voters at York Castle to report that in that election one of the candidates whom they returned was the one who could afford the least amount of inducement money, namely the saintly Wilberforce whose main object was to rescue thousands of slaves whom Yorkshiremen could never see.

However, in October 1812 the three candidates were Lord Milton, son of Earl Fitzwilliam; Mr Lascelles, son of the Earl of Harewood; and Mr Wortley, who hadn't such a prestigious name but was popular with some of the citizens of York. Each of them wrote letters to the papers trying to drum up support and they appeared at a preliminary meeting of Forty-Shilling Freeholders in the Castle Yard, as the Eye of York was then called. The King's Writ for convening a new Parliament was read, followed by the Act for Preventing Bribery and Corruption – not that the latter was likely to have much effect.

The High Sheriff of Yorkshire had the job of asking for nominations; then two gentlemen proposed respectively Viscount Milton and the Hon. Henry Lascelles. Immediately voices shouted, 'Wortley! Wortley!'

Their protegé stepped forward and disappointed them. He wouldn't stand. '. . . however much gratified I might be by this proof of your regard, I thought it my duty to retire. I know no man better able than myself to appreciate the situation to which a contested election would have reduced this county; and I should have felt a very serious sense of responsibility, if by any act of mine, however worthy the object, the county had been plunged into a state of confusion.'

With those well-chosen phrases, he saved himself a lot of money and the populace a lot of fun and fisticuffs.

41

The High Sheriff then asked for a show of hands in favour of the remaining two candidates, which he got, and immediately declared 'The Right Honourable Charles William Wentworth Fitzwilliam, Viscount Milton, and the Honourable Henry Lascelles to be duly elected as knights to represent this county in Parliament'.

What price Democracy?

The Debtors' Prison, now part of York Castle Museum.

The New Drop

THINGS WERE NOT ALWAYS JUST what they seemed in Regency York. The houses at the bottom end of Castlegate appeared elegant, they were comfortably appointed and furnished with considerable expense. Moreover, the inhabitants were said to have one of the best situations in the town. One had Clifford's Tower in its garden, another had an extensive collection of shrubs, a third had gardens sloping down to the River Foss. Yet they were only a very short walk from one of the most depressing and degrading areas of the city.

And even that looked good on the outside. For York Castle, as it was still named, comprised no dungeons or battlements but three palatial-looking buildings designed to look like the homes of wealthy Venetian aristocrats. In fact, they were two prisons and the Law Court. Some people claimed that the prison at York Castle was one of the best in Europe. If it was, the rest must have been appalling beyond description.

Standing with your back to Clifford's Tower today, you can still see the 18th-century Law Courts on your right but the other buildings now house one of the most interesting museum collections in Britain. In Regency days, however, the one on your left was the women's prison and the noble-looking façade facing you was the gaol for debtors and male felons.

York Prison (now the York Castle Museum).

Anyone seriously in debt was confined until he paid his creditors, a self-defeating measure which effectively prevented the man from repaying what he owed because it deprived him of the means to go out and earn a living. Some of them made small items for sale and, since the public were allowed to wander in the courtyard, the debtors had permission to set out their handicrafts there and sell them to visitors. They must have been glad of the fresh air for the prison was notoriously evil-smelling, although the debtors were kept in rooms above the Governor's residence and didn't experience the worst that York Castle could offer. Even if the debtor managed to secure his release with the aid of gifts from his family and friends, he needed enough to pay the obligatory sum demanded by the gaoler and turnkeys from all prisoners on their departure.

The prison staff didn't get wages; they were expected to make a profit from supplying the needs of their charges. Prisoners were not provided with anything except a loaf of bread a day and a shilling a week. They could have anything else they fancied – provided they paid for it. Wine, chicken, feather mattresses and comfortable chairs, coal for the fire, books to read and the company of family or friends; everything was permitted to those who could afford it. Turnkeys fetched what was desired and charged more than its cost, thereby securing their own livelihood. But even the most well-to-do prisoner couldn't buy immunity from 'gaol fever', the dreaded typhus which was rampant in prisons with water as contaminated as that in York Castle. Yet the debtor could try to keep personally clean for the inmates of the Women's Prison did the washing for debtors.

Even political misdemeanours could get a man into the gaol where he led the same sort of dreary existence as the debtors. James Montgomery, writer of the Christmas carol: *Angels from the Realms of Glory*, was one of these prisoners and enlivened his long hours writing amusing poems. In one of them he refers to the prison clock (still visible above the gaol) which didn't always keep reliable time:

> How gaily spins the weather-cock!
> How proudly shines the crazy clock!
> A clock, whose wheels eccentric run,
> And yet it shows us, right or wrong,
> The days are only twelve hours long;
> Though captives often reckon here
> Each day a month, each month a year.

And yet the conditions of debtors were princely in comparison to those of the 'misdemeanants' or 'felons' as they were called. The fact that these were allowed soap was regarded as a generous concession and it was thought to be rather wonderful that, in the interests of cleanliness, the place was whitewashed twice a year. Not that this would be much comfort to those kept in solitary confinement; the visitor to the Castle Museum may still see the tiny, dark cells kept for this purpose. Even that doesn't give a clear impression of the misery experienced here for it doesn't show the casual tourist the early 19th-century prisoner in his irons, scantily clad – some of them without a shirt.

It was the gaol which caused York to receive a visit from one of the most famous Englishwomen; Elizabeth Fry came here in 1819.

Her relation and companion, Joseph Gurney, recorded the scenes which met her serene eyes. 'The prisoners are allowed one pound and a half of wheaten bread daily . . . From the squalid appearance of some of them, it seemed to us questionable whether the allowance of food was sufficient to maintain them in health; the apothecary of the prison, whom we saw, expressed an opinion that it was not.'

The magistrates were responsible for the administration of the prison and when they read Joseph Gurney's description of Elizabeth's findings, they were incensed. The fact that unscrupulous people in York were pawning the prisoners' clothes didn't enhance the reputation of the Justices. They were horrified when Gurney's account was published and the world could read that felons were sometimes incarcerated in small rooms where no daylight could reach and compelled to sleep two in a bed and to spend their days weighted down with irons and without anything interesting or useful to do. Joseph Gurney thought they should be taught a trade to equip them for an honest life when they came out of prison.

The magistrates wrote a reply to his criticism which was printed by Mr Storry in Petergate. Part of its long-winded title stated that it was 'occasioned by an unfavourable representation, made in a late publication of the state of that prison'. It didn't convince Mr Gurney who returned to the prison and found that no improvements had taken place. He was accompanied by Samuel Tuke, one of the altruistic Quakers who took a leading part in the life of Regency York.

In fact, imprisonment was not a very common punishment but that doesn't mean there weren't plenty of people in prison. Most of them were awaiting trial for offences which would be penalised by fines, corporal punishment, transportation or death. Some were acquitted, but they had meanwhile endured conditions which surely had a lasting effect on their minds. No one in those days spoke of nervous breakdowns but they must have suffered from them. The period of remand varied, not according to the seriousness of the alleged crime, but according to how soon a visiting judge would come to hold the Assizes.

When the learned gentleman arrived, he stayed in the Judge's Lodging, a house still in Lendal, which is now a hotel. The neighbouring gentry and some of the aristocracy then came to stay in their town houses and take part in the balls, assemblies, races and theatrical performances put on to mark the Assizes. The judge made his stately progress to the Law Courts and the prison population dwindled as one was sent to Van Dieman's Land (Tasmania) as a convict, another was whipped and released, another hanged. If the prison was very overfull, the JPs sometimes asked for a special Assize 'for purposes of Gaol Delivery' and the local inhabitants had all the fun of a few extra dances and plays whilst the luckless prisoners were dispatched.

At the Lent Assizes in 1812 the jury comprised two baronets, three knights, and two sons of peers; the remaining jurors were described as 'esquires' which meant that they were gentlemen who owned land and the names of their homes were given, such as Gladstone House and Newby Park. They were not a very proletarian set! They sat in judgement upon such people as a highwayman and a carpenter accused of cutting down an ash tree and stealing its wood.

Another defendant was William Chester who was charged 'by the oath of George Oliver of Apleton-le-Street in the North Riding, innkeeper, with having between one and two o'clock on Monday morning the 14th instant, burglariously entered his house and attempted to murder him and his wife'.

Thomas Hawke was tried for bigamy and sentenced to be privately whipped and imprisoned for six months.

The gaol wasn't empty after the Assizes were over; the debtors remained, plus a few convicted men whose sentence was imprisonment. These included some rioters from Sheffield who were to be kept in York Castle for one year. Not all sentenced to imprisonment were confined at York; some were moved elsewhere, like William Sands, found guilty of stealing a pocket book and condemned to hard labour in Wakefield House of Correction for two years.

For those, whom the black-capped judge condemned to death, the end was literally in sight. There was no police force to keep the citizens of York in order; the tendency to crime was supposed to be checked by terror of its consequences, so hanging was seen to be done. Castlegate Postern Lane was widened near the city wall to make room for large crowds to gaze with *frissons* of horror at the public executions.

The 'gallow's bird', as contemporaries labelled him, spent his final night in the condemned cell. Tourists may still see this room with its thick walls and iron bedstead in the Debtor's Prison. When the first rays of dawn penetrated the barred window, the convicted man rose to face in his own way the workings of an unpitying law code. Some dressed in their best clothes; others didn't possess such aids to courage. Some joked with bravado or studied nonchalance; others surely found it difficult to walk.

The Condemned Cell at York Castle Museum.

The victim was led out; fresh air fanned his cheeks for the last time. A scaffold called the New Drop (to distinguish it from the old Tyburn on the Knavesmire) had been erected at the back of the Castle and there, accompanied by his own coffin, he stood above a swearing, eating, drinking, shouting crowd as they watched the hangman fasten the noose. One last look towards the fields and trees which bordered the river and then the platform was removed and he was 'launched into Eternity'.

In 1812, it is comforting to note, only one person was sentenced to death and this was commuted to imprisonment whilst John Waddingham, a highwayman, who wisely pleaded guilty, was merely imprisoned for six months. The authorities were not always so merciful.

In January 1813 York was buzzing with talk about the Luddites, men who got their nickname from a fictitious leader, Ned Ludd. They were machine-busters who feared that new inventions would destroy their livelihood. In many factories, jobs were now being done by machinery and people like handloom weavers were unemployed. A gang of young men, who'd attacked the mill belonging to a Mr Cartwright, had been arrested near Huddersfield and brought to York Castle for trial because it was the County Court.

The *York Chronicle* gave a vivid account of the night when Mr Cartwright, staying in the mill with some of his men and five soldiers to protect it from a Luddite attack, experienced just that. The alarm was given by his big dog. Downstairs windows were shattered as young Luddites broke into the building. Mr Cartwright and his men grabbed weapons and started ringing the warning bell at the top of the mill. It didn't deter the attackers who hurled stones and shot at the factory, egged on by a mob of supporters shouting, 'Bang up, lads, in with you, keep close, damn that bell, get to it, damn 'em, kill 'em all'. The bell rope broke and in a 20 minute fight pistols, muskets, mill-stones, hatchets, hammers and sticks were frantically used.

All this was reported in York's County Court and the jury were shown in evidence a dark mask and a water-stained hat pulled out of the mill pond. The 'Learned Judge', Sir Simon le Blanc summed up and gave his advice to the jury who retired to consider their verdict.

It only took them an hour. They were a crop of 12 Yorkshire landowners who don't seem to have spent long weighing pros and cons but, to their credit, they did consider the accused individually and not condemn them *en masse*. They even found James Brook, John Brook and John Hirst not guilty. (James Brook had been having a traumatic time recently. He'd lost a £1 promissory note and some silver and copper coins to men who threatened him and who now stood trial for that offence.)

For the rest of the accused the verdict was: Guilty.

Now the judge put on his black cap and his legal phrases fell on a hushed court. 'Thou shalt be hanged by the neck until the body be dead.'

York people discussed the case in the streets and in their houses. There were not many in those days who disagreed with the death penalty and there were lots who thought private property was absolutely sacred and anyone attacking it got no more than he deserved. This opinion was not necessarily shared by those who never had any property nor by the influential and gentler Quaker fraternity.

There were plenty of spectators on the morning when the men were led out to the New Drop. All the condemned were married, one had a pregnant wife, and more than 50 children would be orphaned that morning.

The prison bell tolled, telling those who had no desire to watch just what was being done at the Castle; guards in the Sheriff's livery took up position round the scaffold. At the Castle gates mounted and foot soldiers were on duty and round the execution platform, their scarlet coats made a splash of bloody colour against the grey January scene.

The men came out to die in two batches.

The giddy clock on the Debtors Prison struck eleven as the first seven were seen walking from their cells to the New Drop; you could hear their voices singing hymns. They arrived at the spot above crowd level, said prayers with a clergyman, and then one of them, Joseph Crowther, turned to the crowd, many of them now shocked and tense. 'Farewell lads!' he shouted.

His comrade, John Hill, made a speech, beginning, 'Friends, all take warning by my fate!' The authorities liked these awful warnings.

More prayers followed and then the hangman's noose.

The next prisoners came out at half past one; they'd had to endure a couple of hours waiting after their comrades had been killed. There were seven of them. The spectators heard them speak of remorse and warn the crowd, which must have included many men tempted by poverty to burglary, not to follow their example.

The mobile platform fell and so, the *Chronicle* reported, 'They were launched into eternity'.

Then, too late, the watching crowd felt pity for the victims.

Condemned Prisoner.

49

What Weather!

It began with the Big Bang, on Christmas Day 1813. York people escaped the worst but heard about the unseasonable thunderstorm which struck Leeds (literally) with such ferocity that two women were injured. Then the great frost set in.

On January 3, 1814 the snow started and didn't seem to know how to stop. By the 6th the thermometer had dropped to 30°F and a few days later there were 22 degrees of frost. People watched the icy river and remembered the fun of skating on it during the freeze of 1807. On this occasion, however, dire warnings were given; seven boys had drowned in the Trent through walking on thin ice and York parents were adjured to watch their children carefully.

On Wednesday morning, the 19th, the stage coach left London for York as usual. Snow started in the South and, as the High Flyer rattled and rumbled into the Midlands, the North wind screamed towards it whipping the snow into drifts and making the coachman long to reach the security of Etteridge's Hotel in York. He got there on the Thursday evening with his feet chilled and his greatcoat covered in snow.

The mail coach was less fortunate. It left Lombard Street on Wednesday evening but on Saturday it still hadn't arrived in York. The snow continued to fall heavily, deadening sound, covering wheel tracks and hiding the hedges which bordered the road. An unlucky coachman could drive over them into a field. Eventually the road was blocked and the mail could go no farther. Some distance behind, Thursday's mail coach was also trapped and the coachman hadn't seen the southbound mail which was delayed in a white world sparkling with silver frost.

Eventually, on Monday evening four mails arrived in York carrying between them 36 bags of letters, which shows just how deep the snow and how ferocious the wind were because, in Regency times, the mails were not normally late, not even by minutes. If anyone in York doubted the church clock, he could set his watch by the arrival of the mail coach in St Helen's Square. The up-coach passed the down-coach at the same place and time on the road each night and, if they were late without good cause, the guard was fined out of his wages. If he got stuck in a snowdrift, he was supposed to cut one of the horses free and ride off with the sacks of mail;

Coach in the Snow.

never mind about the passengers, they didn't matter. But even this Draconian rule was useless if snow was piled so deeply as in the January of 1814.

By January 23 there were 16 inches of snow lying on the ground and no one could recall seeing it so deep previously. People were just like us – trying to find precedents and reasons for the harsh weather. Some said it was due to 'the retrocession of the lunar nodes', believing that when the moon's path crossed that of the sun it upset the weather. This, they decided, accounted also for the severe winter of 1794-5 when the French with all their artillery crossed frozen rivers in Holland. Perhaps, someone suggested hopefully, frozen rivers would now give the Dutch a chance to expel the 'French imperialists'. At any rate Yorkshiremen could walk across the frozen Ouse in places.

As fresh snow clouds were driven in from the west adding more depth to the whitened fields and moors, it might have prevented the mails from getting to York at all. However, by this time the Government was finding ways of dealing with the problem. The Prince Regent gave orders that where necessary the mail bags should be carried over the snow-laden fields in chaises drawn by six horses. There were posting houses in York, such as Etteridge's on the site of the present Thomas's Hotel. These inns supplied 'yellow bounders' at a cost. It is the measure of Britain's pride in her unique postal service that such an expensive method of delivering the mail should be used.

In the chilly conditions potatoes became severely frost-bitten and people tried new ways of cooking them to make them more palatable. They boiled them and then, after they'd gone cold, they roasted them.

In the teeth of a bitter nor'-easter, which blew constantly for several days, emaciated figures in patched garments and leaking shoes, crept close to the wall of the Bedern. The affluent citizens began to feel disturbed consciences and gave donations to help the poor. Then a smug self-satisfaction healed the disturbed consciences and the newspaper commented on the 'mercy and compassion which have ever been associated with the British name' and which 'have greatly distinguished our humane and benevolent countrymen on the late distressing occasion'. Perhaps it was not the fault of York's more fortunate citizens but a number of elderly people died as a result of the intense cold. There was no national pension scheme.

Everyone was aware that the ground was frozen to a depth of several inches so it couldn't absorb the melted snow when the thaw came. The rivers of the Pennines poured into the Ouse and the river burst its banks, flooding the countryside and York. It saturated the gardens of Coney Street houses and flooded the Guildhall cellars. The King's Arms could only admit customers who were willing to paddle in its tap room. The water reached up into Skeldergate and many people would have had flooded homes. At last the thaw made it easier to bring coal up river again reducing its high price.

Woman with donkey outside Bedern Chapel.

York versus 'Boney'

THE BRITISH AND FRENCH FOUGHT each other with swords, muskets, rifles, carronades and cannon for almost 22 years. The British Army, commanded by Wellington, spent nearly seven of those bloody years in Spain trying to drive the French out of it. This long campaign is the famous Peninsular War.

Napoleon (variously called here the Monster, the Ogre, the Corsican and other ruder names) dominated the Continent until his final defeat at Waterloo.

When Johnny came marching home again to York, he'd probably be wearing the uniform of one of two Yorkshire regiments present at Waterloo – the 33rd and the 51st Regiments of the Line. Both wore the British red coat but the facings of collar and cuffs and the plume on his shako told the initiated which regiment the hero belonged to.

However, most York men didn't volunteer for the professional army but they might find themselves in the militia. In some ways the militia was a kind of Dad's Army of the 19th century. It got its recruits by a system of ballot; from time to time men received a number and if that number turned up in the ballot, you either put on a red coat and learned to fire a musket or you paid another fellow £29 odd to take your place. At least the militia didn't get sent farther away from York than Ireland. A lot of time was spent in marching and counter-marching whilst the locals admired the smartness of drill and uniforms, but these were genuine patriots, willing to give their lives if Boney should land.

Which fortunately he didn't. In 1811 the *York Chronicle* said that the Government would only call out the militia for 14 days training. Next year Boney invaded Russia and a ballot was held to fill the spare places in the local militia.

War news reached the York population in the newspapers which printed Wellington's despatches, but obviously these took some time to arrive. Most people learned of allied victories when a stage coach arrived from London decorated with ribbons and banners whilst the coachman waved his whip and shouted the good news as he drove down Micklegate and along Coney Street. Later it was possible to read the details because Lord Liverpool, the Prime Minister from 1812, sent an account which

British Soldier

included lists of killed and wounded to the Lord Mayor who passed it to the local press. Almost every copy of the newspapers contained war news, so there was hardly a week when the citizens did not read about such matters as naval battles, French troop movements in Europe or rumours of an attack in Ireland.

Some accounts gave exciting news of individual men. A description of the escape of Lieut. Jackson RN from a French fortress where he was a prisoner-of-war finished with this comment: 'Here we have the genuine seeds of deeds of glory, which cherished under the fostering care of a Nelson and a Wellington, have already produced such achievements of military skill and prowess, under favour of Divine Providence, as no other nation in the universe can boast.'

In April 1812 the details of the siege of Badajoz in Spain were printed. This included lists of killed and wounded which must have been read with great apprehension, although church bells would ring to announce another victory.

No one, rejoicing in York, could see the charred remains of British soldiers in the breach at Badajoz; no one, congratulating himself on our troops' triumph at Spanish Vitoria, could hear the painful gasps of dying Redcoats on that battlefield; no one, reading in his paper of the army's miraculous march over the Pyrenees, could imagine the British soldiers climbing above the snow line with a handful of acorns for their dinner. Without television coverage and with no journalists accompanying the forces, Britons basked in self-approval. They were right in believing that their men were brave but their concepts of war were seldom based on first-hand knowledge. So they pictured a well-fed British 'Johnny' with a cringing Frenchman at his heel. They hadn't seen the courage with which the 'Froggies' died for their emperor; they hadn't seen the faded red jackets and the trousers made of old blankets, hastily cobbled together, which covered men who had 'taken the King's shilling' because they were desperately poor and the army was a job.

Yet the York gentleman, reading his newspaper beside a crackling fire, was not entirely wrong in his assessment, for the letters and diaries of men serving in the army and navy reflect immense confidence and pride. Before Badajoz the men were actually hoping that it would not surrender without needing to be attacked. One of them wrote, '. . . there were, perhaps, not three men in the three divisions who would not rather have braved all the chances than receive it tamely from the hands of the enemy'.

When the Waterloo campaign started everyone knew that the army, which had won so many encounters against French generals in the Peninsula, would be facing Napoleon himself this time. When Wellington had fought the French in Spain, Napoleon had been fighting elsewhere in Europe and his marshals lacked his brilliance as a commander. But the British considered that the Duke of Wellington was his equal. Before nearly every one of Wellington's victories there had been a thunderstorm and on the day before Waterloo there was a monumental storm; Peninsula veterans were delighted and watched Wellington with confidence. An officer wrote, 'The sight of his long nose among us was worth ten thousand men'.

It needed to be. Those who returned to York after Waterloo had tales of horror and heroism to repeat. The battle was so fiercely fought that more than one man wrote that he actually wondered if it could result in every man being killed.

The Redcoats formed squares whilst enemy cavalry attacked them; they stood for a long time enduring a cannonade which killed and wounded their friends beside them, they simply removed the body and shuffled across the narrow space to close the gap. The 33rd Regiment, formed in Yorkshire, was a special favourite with Wellington who had once been its colonel. In the heat of conflict he asked their brigade commander how they were. The reply was that two-thirds of them had fallen and the rest were so tired that they needed to have some other troops to take their place. But Wellington explained that, if they were to be seen withdrawing, it would endanger the battle. 'Enough, my lord, we stand here until the last man falls,' replied the brigade commander, Sir Colin Halkett. And so they stood, their red coats and green shako plumes smutty and greyed from gun smoke, until the final victorious charge. They had lost 269 out of their 561 men.

Captain Robert Wallace, who was a well-known resident of York, described how, when his regiment charged, he saw a French trumpeter lying on the stubble ground; nearly all the men charging past on horseback slashed at him with their swords. Wallace said, 'I did not slash at him, but the trumpeter slashed at me!'

Troop Sergt-Maj. Thomas Nicholson got a sabre wound whilst he was in a charge at Waterloo and was discharged from the army. He came to live in York and kept the inn called the Light Horseman in Fulford Road. Men coming home to York must have found difficulty adjusting to everyday life; they had taken part in one of the most famous battles of all time.

It was not surprising that people in York collected subscriptions for the families of those who fell at Waterloo. For several weeks the *York Courant* gave lists of all those who had contributed and the amount they had given with the total collected at the time of going to press. When all York's best-known citizens had been recorded, the various villages in the locality sent in their collections.

Nothing was too bad to say about Napoleon apparently and we know that York people discussed his meanness in not allowing the British Government to provide basic necessities for its prisoners-of-war incarcerated in the infamous fortress of Bitche. His relationship with his divorced wife, Josephine, was a subject of juicy gossip in York.

Finally in 1816 the West York Militia Corps were disembodied (ie. disbanded) at York. Meanwhile Napoleon had been sent into exile on St Helena; but even in that Atlantic island he was not safe from the vituperation of York's press which told its readers: 'Bonaparte every day grows more and more sullen in his demeanour . . .'

A Shako worn at Waterloo.

XII

Promise to Pay

IN 1811 JOHN WALTON WAS COMMITTED to York Castle for 'having feloniously forged a certain promissory note to the amount of forty-one pounds'.

What had he actually done? He'd forged something rather like a cheque. A person whose money was deposited in a bank might write an order to the bank to pay a specified sum out of their savings to another individual, who could then take that 'promissory note' to the bank and get it cashed. Alternatively he could give the note itself to a third party who could take it to the bank and obtain the cash. In this way promissory notes became a kind of currency.

Throughout the French wars we suffered from a lack of metal for making coins. This led to many different methods of payment and it's a wonder that people understood them all. Due to the shortage of specie, it became a criminal offence to send gold out of the country and York citizens were reminded in their weekly paper of the penalties for doing this; also that if they informed on anyone exporting gold, they would be rewarded with one-third of the value of the gold.

These were not the days of the Big Five clearing banks. In the early 19th century there were many privately-owned banks; York had three. Messrs Raper, Swann and Company were on the corner of New Street and Coney Street. Messrs Wilson Sons and Company had premises in High Ousegate almost opposite All Saints lantern church. Messrs Godfrey and Wentworth started a bank in 1812 beside the bridge at the bottom of Low Ousegate; they had smart new premises because the old houses there had been demolished to widen the approach to Ouse Bridge.

The nearest thing to a computer, which any of these banks owned, was a counting-house full of ledgers and clerks sharpening quill pens, whilst they totted up beautifully written columns of figures. For the hours and hours spent beside a leatherbound account book and a pewter inkstand, the clerk would do well if he got an annual salary of much more than £20.

It was safer to deposit money in a York bank than to keep it at home in those policeless days. There would be a strong room on the premises and many bankers kept pistols to protect their customers' money and their own gold reserves.

Some banks issued their own notes, a helpful practice when the country was short of coins. The banknote was printed with the phrase we still use: 'I promise to pay . . .' and the words meant what they said. The note could be exchanged for cash at the bank, but alternatively it could be passed to someone else in payment of a debt and the new possessor of it could present it at the local bank for cash payment. In practice most people didn't bother to swap the note for coins and so the banknotes became currency like the promissory notes. Most folk relied on the local banker's ability to produce 'real money' if necessary and accepted the notes happily, even preferring them to those of the Bank of England, although they would be suspicious of notes from some country bank in an area they didn't know. Godfrey and Wentworth issued their own notes at their premises in Low Ousegate. Their £1 note had a picture of York Minster in one corner but was plain white on the other side.

Popular as their notes were in York, they wouldn't be well-known in London, so they had a London agent (called Wentworth and Company) who was willing to accept their notes and give their value in coinage to anyone who presented them. This gave York people somewhere to bank in London if they endured the 20-odd hours' journey to the capital.

During the war some people were afraid to use paper money issued by small banks and there could be a panicky run of folk taking their notes to be cashed. Disaster occurred if that bank hadn't kept enough cash to honour all of them. Quite a number of banks 'went bust', but this didn't happen to the York banks.

Sometimes travellers carried a strong box in their carriage and might have servants who were armed to protect them from highway robbery. The more intrepid passengers kept a pistol in their coach ready to use it themselves if a masked figure appeared. Of course, banknotes were a safer way to take a lot of money on a long journey; they were also lighter. Coins could be heavy; the 'cartwheel twopence' was well named for it was solid copper and bigger than our 50 pence piece. A pocketful of those would soon have pulled a pair of skin-tight pantaloons into a very odd shape, but most men carried a purse for their loose change.

Or they could use a pocket book for notes. When one of these was lost, Raper and Co offered a reward of £20 for its recovery – not a very princely sum seeing that their client's pocket book contained six £10 notes and one £5 issued by a Doncaster bank, a £1 note from a Leeds bank and four £2 Bank of England notes.

The design of the York banknotes was quite elaborate but it was impossible to prevent forgery altogether. The Government aimed to prevent illegal notes by the stiff penalties available to judges. It could be a hanging matter, so the forger at Brighton who was merely imprisoned for six months got a mention in the York newspaper.

The papers were usually a good source of fiscal news, everything from prices on the Stock Exchange to details of the latest bankrupt could be read there. Creditors would look in the *Chronicle* or *Herald* to find when the man owing them money would appear. He would usually come on two different dates to local inns and give a list of all his assets so a commissioner could be appointed who would share out those assets between all the creditors. The poor bankrupt himself would probably end up in York Castle prison and his next communication with the public would be through the grating in the wall.

Old York Bank Note, 1817.

XIII

York's Liquid Asset

THE SILVER RIBBON OF THE OUSE, which brought goods and trade to the city, also divided York and only one bridge connected the hub of the town with the main road to the rest of England. This was the old Ouse Bridge, a hump-backed, five-arched medieval structure, which was about to be replaced in the year the Regency began. Already the church at the Micklegate end of it had been demolished to make way for the new bridge designed by Peter Atkinson the younger.

About time, too; traffic jams in York are not an invention of the 20th century for the old bridge was too narrow for two big vehicles to get by. The farm waggons, stage coaches and lumbering eight-horse drawn waggons with iron hoops and canvas awning covering their goods, could hardly pass. No doubt loud-voiced expletives rent the air as drivers tried to push their teams up the steep incline in opposition to the coachman coming from the other way. Yet this was the main link between the West and East Ridings of Yorkshire. It must often have been said that the vague 'They' ought to do something about it.

Proposed new Ouse Bridge.

'They' did – and ran into money problems which made the job take nearly 10 years to complete. Meanwhile the bridge was too necessary to be closed. Instead the upstream side was rebuilt first, allowing traffic to use the south side; in 1817 the first pedestrians were able to walk along the north part of the bridge we see today. No one looked forward to the day when they would have to pay tolls to drive over the finished bridge but the prospect of those tolls was the main security for borrowing enough money to build the new structure.

Investors bought shares in lots of £50 and were informed that 'Whoever is willing to advance the said money or any part thereof, may apply to Messrs R. Townend and Bayldon, at their office in Brearey Court, York, who will pay the interest regularly half-yearly'.

York made plenty of use of the Ouse; people fished it, sailed it and drank it. Lendal Tower was heightened to contain a tank; a Newcomen steam engine, clanking and hissing, pumped water up to it, not that there was ever enough for the town's needs.

Ferrymen, with rowing boats, took passengers across the water and probably did a good trade when the bridge was half-closed for rebuilding.

A large crane dominated the wharf at the lower end of Skeldergate. Other cranes were needed for emptying cargo from the various ships and boats which plied the river. There was a longer stretch of natural bank than there is now and it often became very muddy. People owning property there received an annual payment for permission for boats to be hauled from the bank, provided gates were shut after use and winches didn't cause inconvenience. Sometimes this towing was done by strong barge horses capable of pulling at least 20 tons burden of craft as it made its way slowly (about two to four miles an hour) upstream. Sometimes the incoming craft were bow-hauled by gangs of men, sweating and straining along the muddy bank. Great square-sailed Humber keels, clinker-built, might be seen coming up from Hull, heavily laden with coal which was unloaded at Old Crane Wharf and Marygate to be taken away in carts.

Two-masted brigs were more common and they enjoyed the traditional right of stopping by the Archbishop's palace for a free beer *en route* for the city.

At the bottom of Marygate a shipbuilding yard provided jobs for skilled men and, amongst other timber, undoubtedly used plenty of elm because it simply hardened in the water making it excellent for parts below the waterline. The word 'elm' aroused emotions in York in 1816 when it was proposed to fell the elm trees which lined the New Walk, a popular riverside promenade. The Lord Mayor received a petition from 'one hundred and forty respectable inhabitants' against this and the trees remained.

It is not surprising that inland navigation was popular at a time when travel by coach was subject to overturns, runaway teams, drunken drivers and highwaymen. Some goods arrived in York by water from as far away as London and the Ouse was the best route to Selby.

As the unladen barge left Marygate for its slow journey, the bargee had plenty of time to look at York from the river. First on his left he'd see the grassy slope below St Mary's Abbey and, if he heard a not-too-distant moo, it came from the cows which ranged among the ruins. As he approached the Lendal and Barker Towers, he would watch out for the ferryboat which carried passengers across the river. Next he passed the Guildhall, its long cream reflections distorted in the rippling grey-brown water.

On the west bank the spire of All Saints, North Street, pencilled the sky and a cobbled path sloped down to the sandy shore. The east bank was lined with stone foundations and the tower of St Martin-le-Grand dominated the horizon. Today silver ripples disturb the reflections from the backs of shops but our Regency bargee would see shrubs and grass in the gardens of Coney Street buildings such as St Martin's vicarage. Wooden scaffolding and builders with hods signalled his arrival at Ouse Bridge and he passed carefully under one of its arches. As the crowd of small boys pointed at his vessel, another might be unloading coal at the small staith on the west bank which hadn't yet got its modern name and was, not unnaturally, often called Coal Staith.

On his left ancient timbered houses overhung the King's Staith and Water Lane terminated here bringing loaded carts to the river bank. If he wasn't tempted to stop and satisfy his thirst at the King's Arms (still here) his craft would glide on past Cumberland House, an imposing dwelling which had got its name from the visit to York of Butcher Cumberland after the Battle of Culloden. There were still some elderly people alive who remembered the visit of this general, George III's uncle, after whom the flower Sweet William was named; not surprisingly the Scots renamed it Stinking Billy. Our bargee was probably not interested in Jacobites or Hanoverians and his eye would stray to the New Wharf on the opposite bank. At busy times the wharf became a place of kegs and casks and rope where men heaved the cargo and patient draught horses pulled it along the quayside.

The bargee couldn't allow his gaze to wander long from the water itself for, besides the flat-bottomed boats called lighters, he might find a brig and a schooner bearing down upon him. If there was a light wind blowing straight down the river, the brig would probably outsail the schooner. Although both were two-masted and carrying a small cargo, the brig was square-rigged which meant it could hang its sails at right-angles to the

deck, letting the breeze fill them. The schooner was fore-and-aft rigged so
its sails hung more limply. Nevertheless, the advantage often lay with the
schooner since the prevailing wind is westerly and frequently shivers
across the water from bank to bank.

First Water Lane.

As his barge glided farther downstream, the bargee came level with Baile Hill and Skeldergate Postern on his right. Here winches and pulleys hoisted and lifted at the Old Wharf and a ferryboat, fastened to an iron ring in the quayside, bobbed up and down. On his left the bargeman passed the city wall and looked across the grass to the great curtain wall still shielding the castle precincts.

He sailed slowly by St George's Field to the confluence where the Foss enters the Ouse. Here the wooden Blue Bridge (named from the colour they'd painted it) allowed people to walk across to the tree-lined promenade where fashionable York sauntered, doffing tall beaver hats and showing off the new Cottage Bonnets and chinchilla tippets purchased in Coney Street.

Now the bargee could look over his shoulder for a last glimpse of the city of medieval towers and brick terraces before he sailed on to Naburn.

The crews of cargo boats and barges were not the only men to sail downstream to Naburn. The newspaper reported a ceremonial procession by York's Corporation, which was thought to be quite a treat for the local inhabitants. The dignitaries were making the annual expedition to maintain their fishing rights and they took a band to enliven the journey with music. On the way back they dined at Naburn Lock House and the paper recorded that the dinner 'was served up with a profusion of wines of the best quality. The day was spent with the utmost harmony and hilarity. A great number of both sexes from the neighbouring village attended, and were highly gratified with the liberal attention of the Corporation in permitting them to share in the festivities of the day'.

There was enormous excitement in April 1816 when word spread through the town that a boat would be coming up-river which didn't depend on wind or muscle. This steam boat, with the topical name of *Waterloo*, was due to leave Hull and come via Selby and Naburn to York. It was only 13 years since the first of these vessels had appeared on the Clyde and they were still rare. Most people called them 'Smoke-boats' because of the belching chimney between the sails. *The Waterloo* was due at 11 o'clock and York citizens streamed to the New Walk to wait for its arrival.

Eleven o'clock came and went; no smoke boat appeared. Several thousand people waited – some certain that it would arrive soon, others probably sure that such a dangerous invention would never make it all the way from Hull to York. There was plenty of time for young men and boys to tell everyone who would listen, and some who wouldn't, all the mechanical details about *The Waterloo*. She was 76 feet long, her engine weighed 25 tons and she had cost £2,600 to build. Older people no doubt said they'd feel safer in the Royal Pilot, a new coach which had started that very week and actually made the whole journey from York to Liverpool in one day!

Half-past twelve came and so did the steam boat, confounding the head-shakers and exciting everyone else. Eager people ran to the edge of the bank to see their first ever steam boat. A tall chimney exuded smoke and a paddle at each side churned water.

All exclamations were silenced by a loud report. *The Waterloo* was armed with swivel guns and her enthusiastic sailors were showing the folk of York that they worked! They were there to protect the mail for this was a packet boat.

Its deck was crowded with passengers; some of them had gone down the river to meet it and now returned triumphantly on board.

The Waterloo came closer, churning her way upstream. Another swivel gun went off but the crowd remained, neck-stretching to see the bow-wave curl round the forepart. Here the light glittered round a jingoistic figurehead; it was Britannia grasping the chained eagle of Napoleonic France and over it the Union Jack was 'triumphantly waving' according to one spectator.

Water lapped the sides as the boat sailed past with its full complement of passengers who had paid for the privilege of being the first people to sail into York under steam. Many of them were sitting below in the best cabin, with panelled walls and crimson-upholstered seats. There was a brass stove to keep them warm, an oil cloth under their feet and refreshments which they could buy.

As oohs and ahs on the bank greeted *The Waterloo*, it splashed past and the watchers could see on the stern a bust of the Duke of Wellington surrounded by 'trophies of victory' with another Union flag waving overhead.

The steam packet continued on its way to York and straining eyes watched its arrow-shaped wake whilst people hurried along the bank behind it. There was going to be a chance to go on board when it anchored in the town.

The privileged Corporation had another treat to come, for the Lord Mayor, his lady, their family and friends were taken back to Naburn on *The Waterloo* at the astonishing speed of 12 miles in less than two hours – and even then, they were told, the boat could have gone faster!

Mind and Spirit

IF YOU WANTED A GOOD READ, you went to York's Subscription Library which was situated in St Helen's Square and doubtless contained all the novels of the day from Jane Austen's *Sense and Sensibility* to Mrs Radcliffe's *Mysteries of Udolpho*. The ladies in Micklegate drawing rooms, who experienced delicious shudders over *Subterranean Horrors* or the *Demon of Sicily*, might be pleasantly surprised by *Northanger Abbey* where Jane Austen parodies the Gothic horror stories which were so fashionable. The clientele of the library probably included some who had been educated at the school for 'young ladies' located in part of the King's Manor.

But there were plenty of people in Regency York who had never had an opportunity to learn their letters from a horn book nor to imitate the words so beautifully engraved in a copy book. Education was not compulsory for anyone and not free for many. Attempts by genuinely well-meaning people, headed by Joseph Lancaster, to give education to poor children successfully increased literacy. Less well-meaning persons established schools intended to make 'The Poor' useful. They would teach a girl knitting but not poetry. A knitting servant could be a domestic advantage but there was no need to stuff her head full of advanced ideas. However, the majority of poor boys still got their 'education' on the streets, learning to beg, sweep chimneys, avoid punishment and touch their caps respectfully.

Some scholastic foundations were the result of a bequest. Dorothy Wilson made a very unusual one; her money was to provide a home for old ladies and a school for boys on the same piece of land. You can still see the building beside the Foss Bridge at the beginning of Walmgate. Here the white-capped old ladies had their bed-sits at the front and at the back the boys learned their lessons – or someone tried to make them. It seems a very rare merger, myopic rheumaticky ladies sinking into a gentle decline and loud-voiced teenage boys daring each other to walk along the parapet of the bridge. Perhaps Dorothy Wilson was a wise woman who believed that lively lads are the best antidote to old age – always presuming that nothing could tame a herd of boys, for these were the days of birch rods.

Another unlikely legacy provided a school for poor children who lived in and near the Pavement. The benefactor had been a dancing master (quite

*Foss Bridge &
Dorothy Wilson's
School*

a popular job with the fashion for gavottes and cotillions) and finally danced his way into the prestigious appointment of Sheriff.

Since there were no government-funded schools, the greatest hope for getting out of the poverty-trap was the education provided by an endowed school. And, if you hadn't any children, the safest way of perpetuating your name was to leave money for a school.

Not all these foundations were thriving. A 17th century bequest had established a school in St Mary Bishophill Junior. The hopeful benefactor had left £6.10s per annum to teach poor children 'to read English perfectly'. This laudable intention was being carried on in the Regency by a widow and her daughter who, not surprisingly, were themselves described as 'poor'.

Some free schools were helped from a trust. One thousand, six hundred and fifty pounds had been invested in four per cent stock and the dividend was shared between several schools.

In Monkgate uniformed lasses attended the Grey Coat School. There were 42 pupils and the school was well-financed from a combination of bequests and donations which it shared with its male counterpart, the Blue Coat School. This boys' establishment was situated in St Anthony's Hall, the ancient building which now houses the Borthwick Institute opposite to the timbered Black Swan in Peaseholme Green. There were 52 lads in the school and, if you want to know what a Blue Coat Boy looked like, go to St Helen's Church near Betty's and look in the window on the left of the main door; there he is, in a stained glass blue coat, breeches and stockings. His hair is in a page boy style, and his coat is endearingly only half-buttoned with bits of shirt sticking out. It has to be admitted that the public didn't think much of the output of the Grey and Blue Coat Schools.

Some schools, intended for the poor, took fee-paying pupils as well to make ends meet; even the 'Free School of the Church of St Peter' which, despite its grandiose title, met in a dilapidated ecclesiastical building in St Andrewgate.

The present day pupils of 'Archbishop's' are better-off than their predecessors. In the early 19th century Archbishop Holgate's School existed in Ogleforth but it only had a handful of pupils who didn't learn much because Mr Sandwich, the schoolteacher, suffered from poor health, finally dying in harness two years after the Regency ended.

Some charities ran schools; another was established for the Society of Friends. A Quaker school for girls had to close down in 1812 through staffing difficulties. Roman Catholics could use the Bar Convent which was usually called quite simply 'The Nunnery in Blossom Street'.

On Sundays most Catholics worshiped in Lop Lane on the site of the present St Wilfred's Church. Christian faith found expression in many forms. The Society of Friends had premises off Castlegate and their devotions frequently inspired help for the poor, the imprisoned and the mentally handicapped. Some of the great Quaker families of England lived in York; we can still see the home of one of them in Marygate Lane. The Particular Baptists used a chapel in Grape Lane; the Presbyterians had one facing it. Methodists had a building in Peaseholme Green where older people could tell the new generation all they remembered of Mr Wesley's visits to York.

1816 was the year when the Prince Regent's daughter, Charlotte, in a silver and white gown, became the bride of Prince Leopold of Saxe-Coburg; it also seemed to be a big year for opening chapels in York. The foundation stone was laid for a new Methodist Chapel in Skeldergate whilst the Congregationalists, who had worshipped in Jubbergate sold their premises to the Unitarian Baptists and built a new chapel in Lendal.

Anglicans had a choice of edifices enriched by the skills of medieval craftsmen and the luminosity of ancient glass. St Michael's, Spurriergate, had been embellished with a 'modern' reredos and altar rails still to be seen by those who seek sanctuary from busy streets in its wholefood restaurant.

Domestic servants who came to work in York probably missed their village church, for rural worshippers were accustomed to sing with the village band on Sundays. Its members stood in the church gallery with a variety of instruments. One of them blew the serpent, an appropriately-named long, winding tube which would look quite in place depicted on a snakes and ladders board. There is a serpent in the Castle Museum, which would have been used by one of the village bands in a parish church. Puffing, blowing, scraping, strumming, the instrumentalists made 'a joyful noise unto the Lord'.

The Cathedral Church by W. Hargrove.

Many a little maid, who came to work in a big house in York, probably found it rather dull to sit silently whilst the choir sang tuneless psalms. If you went to the Methodists you might enjoy 'a good sing' of one of the late Mr Charles Wesley's rousing hymns. Then Jonathan Gray, the zealous organist at St Saviour's (and friend of Wilberforce) thought the town congregations should be able to join in the singing so he introduced the hymn book compiled by William Richardson, the curate at St Michael-le-Belfry. During the Regency 30 of York's churches used this book.

Most churches had only one service on the Sabbath. If you went to a Forenoon Church, you were going to a place where the service was on a Sunday morning; in contrast, others were Afternoon Churches.

The Minster itself stood in splendid dignity surrounded by its 'Liberty', a close within walls where ecclesiastical law prevailed. There were even rumours of an underground dungeon there! It gave the readers of Gothic romances terrifying shivers – until the public house above it was demolished in that eventful year 1816. All they found were some oak doors and iron rings, but to the fertile imagination that was enough and they were even described as 'the marks of despotic cruelty'. They produced delicious shudders in fashionable young ladies who walked that way to church but they didn't disturb the tranquility of the faithful kneeling nearby.

Each Sunday, in hearty singing or quiet prayer, with communal responses or mystic silences, the faithful of York sought communion with the Creator of the Universe.

The Sermon.

The Lord Nelson Coach

ANYONE MAKING A TOUR OF ENGLAND in Regency times – and some intrepid travellers did brave potholes, highwaymen and tipsy coachmen to do just that – would probably have included York in their itinerary. There are still extant accounts written by visitors who came North and stayed in England's second city.

They weren't all favourably impressed. One didn't appreciate 'the lingo'; he wrote, 'The common people speak English very ill, and have a strange accented pronunciation of some words, as at hoose, moose, coo, for house, mouse, cow, and so on.'

Another complained that the inhabitants didn't know enough about the place. Encountering a couple of Yorkies sitting on a bench, he plonked himself between them and said undiplomatically, 'I have many questions to ask about York; and I love to apply to old age. Are you natives?'

'Yes.'

'Then you are the people I want.'

He got no satisfactory reply to his questions. This he put down to shocking ignorance but one wonders if there was another reason, especially since he treated them to a superior smile and the comment, 'That a man should live seventy years in a place and not know it! Had I been a native, I should have written its history.' He then went on to stay in Scarborough where he paid £1.5s a week board for himself and his daughter and half as much for his servant, whose board cost the same as that of the horse which also received corn.

Most of York's streets were narrow and lined with Tudor houses whose overhanging upper storeys made them dark, although some of these buildings were light in colour because their oak beams had been covered in fashionable Regency stucco; even St William's College was whitewashed and divided into flats. Some visitors complained that York's narrow roads were airless and one suggested that Tudor dwellings should be pulled down to give more light and space.

Other people complained that the ancient buildings were neglected; some of the stonework from St Mary's Abbey was filched for use in repairing newer houses. Archbishop Markham had a hard job to save parts

Minerva at the Minster end of Stonegate.

of the famous city walls from demolition. Historic cities had not yet learned how to turn their ancient remains into commercial assets, but there were those who liked the atmosphere of medieval and Tudor times which dominated York particularly in the Shambles, still the province of butchers, and Stonegate, a street catering for those with a thirst and those

William Alexander's Bookshop: York Castle Museum.

with intellectual needs. Even then, the Starre Inn advertised its services with a beam stretched across the street. Another sign, that of Minerva the Roman goddess of Wisdom, drew attention to bookshops. She appears on the Museum's version of the Castlegate premises of William Alexander, the Quaker bookseller who was also a publisher and sold leatherbound copies of Hargrove's *History of York* – besides purveying gold paper-hangings and writing desks, parasols and umbrellas made to look like walking canes, and according to his advertisement, 'those with metal tubes in the common forms, and a considerable variety besides in silk and gingham; both of the cheapest kinds and those of SUPERIOR manufacture'. Sir Walter Scott stayed with him in 1819, the year that *Ivanhoe* was published.

There were several booksellers in Stonegate. T. Nicholson, on the corner of Little Stonegate, promised in his advert: 'Schoolmasters supplied on the most reasonable terms.' Next door to a barber-surgeon, whose overhanging house was decorated with elaborate carvings on the timbered front, stood Todd's bookshop. The Todds (father and two sons) followed their trade at 'The Sign of the Bible'. Houses and shops seldom had numbers, so the owners frequently used a wooden sign or figure indicative of their trade. Two of these can still be seen; the Scotsman who once stood by a snuff shop now stands in 'the street' at the Castle Museum whilst Napoleon remains beside the newsagent's in Lendal.

The Todds had a warehouse, its walls lined from floor to ceiling with books lit by skylights. The latest publications were there and antiquarian books, too, for some people sold their private collections to them. It was possible to have the books of your choice bound in leather to match your

Todd's Bookshop in Stonegate.

73

room. Most books were sold without covers so you could select your own binding. Clearly books were often purchased to enhance the décor; if you were having your room redecorated you might like to get a few shelves of volumes bound in brown leather to match the carpet's principal colour – there was no need to *read* them!

Todd's warehouse had a suitably classical air, heightened by the busts and pilasters redolent of ancient Greece or Rome. Its quietly scholastic ambience was in contrast to some of the narrow streets behind it such as Mucky Peg Lane. No one knows for sure about the origin of that name but if Peg acquired the nickname in days when personal hygiene wasn't so popular as now, there was probably a strongly olfactory reason for it.

Another bookseller and publisher, Mr Wolstenholme, worked in the house at the south-west corner of Minster Gates and his Minerva is still in position over the doorway. One may see her by standing at the spot where Petergate crosses Stonegate and looking up to first floor level.

It is now time to find again the imaginary traveller who entered York by stage-coach in our first chapter. He has spent a busy week in this city; now he is going on to Scarborough to get a breath of the North Sea. Let us watch him depart.

He would have to get up early on Monday morning and go to the Black Swan, Mr Clark's hotel in Coney Street, as the Lord Nelson Coach left there at nine o'clock for the Bell and George Inn in Scarborough. He could have gone an hour later from the George in Coney Street but he wouldn't be allowed to take more than £5 worth of luggage on that coach and, having come from London, he'd have many parcels besides those he had bought in York which might include a £6 patent mangle from Gibson, the ironmonger in the Pavement. He probably couldn't resist the manufacturer's description of it: '. . . an ornamental furniture for a gentleman's kitchen, only requiring the strength of a child to work it.'

So he would eat his breakfast early in the York Tavern and stride into St Helen's Square – not that it really was a square, more of a triangle with St Helen's churchyard taking up much of the present space. He must turn the corner into Coney Street; its pavements would still be fairly clean at this hour. York householders had to sweep the pavement in front of their home before sunset or pay a fine of three shillings and fourpence. You had to repair the pavement, too, when it needed, for your £4 rate only enabled the parish to provide lamps, the Charleys and the Workhouse in Marygate; the Corporation gravelled the roads.

Our traveller would be hoping the York Tavern had sent his luggage down to the coach as he'd requested. He arrived at the pillared entrance surmounted by the flamboyant bird with arched neck. Inside the aroma of coffee, beer and beef was as welcoming as the crackling fires which

The Black Swan Inn, Coney Street, York.

warmed the dining and tap rooms. Nowadays, if we visit the British Home Stores, we tread on the ground once covered by the Black Swan. If our fictitious passenger had really bought that mangle, he'd be regretting it. No way could it be accepted on the Lord Nelson, such an encumbrance had to travel on the slow stage waggon starting near All Saints, Pavement.

It would have been wiser to buy his lady a length of jaconet muslin from Welbanks in Minster Yard and some lace from Mrs Ingham on the corner of Spurriergate and Jubbergate. That would have been a valuable gift; John Harbutt (in York City Gaol in 1817) was condemned to death for stealing muslin and lace.

The Lord Nelson could only accommodate four inside passengers but our traveller had booked a seat in there. The fare was 12 shillings whereas the roof was only eight, but he'd probably found that lofty position too cold on the journey from the capital. However, on his return to York he might sit on the roof again. It was all right travelling *to* Scarborough inside but *back* would be different. People were apt to buy fresh fish at the seaside and the inside of a coach was notoriously unpleasant if another passenger was carrying either cheese or fresh fish – it was never fresh by journey's end.

But it was better not to be on the roof in certain areas of York because inn signs overhung the streets dangerously and even pedestrians were wise to step into the middle of the road in some parts, especially if there was a wind blowing. Of course, if he was nervous of travelling, the passenger might have been to Spence and Burdekin to buy some Cordial Balm of Gilead which was sold for 'Nervous consumptions, lowness of spirits and inward decays . . . whether hereditary or owing to youthful imprudencies'. A dose of that before the journey was probably a good idea for its vendors said, '. . . it not only invigorates the decayed juices, but throws a genial warmth upon the debilitated and relaxed parts that stand in need of assistance'.

Perhaps the passenger might be forgiven for being a trifle apprehensive. It required great skill to drive a coach and horses through York's medieval streets, although some local drivers were so accustomed to it that they laughed at the difficulties of newcomers. When the Rev Sidney Smith, the witty incumbent of Foston, complained that there was no room for carriages to pass, a York driver retorted, 'There's plenty of room and over an inch to spare'.

Anyway, the guard would blow a warning blast on his horn as the Lord Nelson swept along Coney Street. The London traveller sat back in his expensive corner; at least this journey would only take seven hours and the road was turnpiked. They rattled through Monk Bar, which still had its barbican, and headed towards the moor whilst whiffs of stagnant odours reached the travellers from the direction of the silted King's Fishpool.

The Londoner looked back at the walled city with its twisted cottages, lantern towers and narrow streets. What an old-fashioned place it was in this year of our Lord, eighteen hundred and eleven! Yet he knew that he was glad he would be coming back to see it again.

Bibliography

Allott, Stephen, *Friends in York*.

Ashton, John, *Social Life Under the Regency*.

Benson, George, *The Theatre Royal and the Drama in York*.

Black, Maggie, *Georgian Meals and Menus*.

Booth, R. K., *York, The History and Heritage of a City*..

Bradley, Tom, *The Old Coaching Days in Yorkshire*.

Cary, *Cary's Roads*, 1819 edition.

Cave, Henry, *Antiquities of York*, 1813 edition.

Chandler, George, *Four Centuries of Banking*.

Cooper, T. P., *The History of the Castle of York*.

Cruikshank, Dan & Burton, Neil, *Life in the Georgian City*.

Dalton, Charles, *The Waterloo Roll Call*.

Digby, Anne, *From York Lunatic Asylum to Bootham Park Hospital*.

Gillett, Edward, *The Humber Region at War 1793-1815*.

Hargrove, William, *History and Description of the Ancient City of York*, 1818 edition.

Heape, R. Grundy, *Georgian York*.

Hutton, W., *A Tour to Scarborough in 1803, Including a Particular Survey of the City of York*.

Johnson, Alan, *The Inns and Alehouses of York*.

Kincaid, Sir J., *Adventures in the Rifle Brigade*, 1830 edition.

Knight, Charles Brunton, *A History of the City of York*.

Knight, Charles Brunton, *This is York*.

Mackintosh, Iain, *The Georgian Playhouse*.

Mee, Arthur, *Yorkshire, East Riding with York*.

Murray, Hugh, Riddick, Sarah and Green, Richard, *York Through the Eyes of the Artist*.

Newman, P. R., *The Royal Castle of York*.

Pevsner, Nikolaus, *Yorkshire, York and the East Riding*.

Potts, John, *York Theatre Royal, 250 Years of Theatre.*

Sessions, William K. & E. Margaret, *Printing in York.*

Sessions, William K. & E. Margaret, *The Tukes of York.*

Temperley, Professor Nicholas, *Jonathan Gray and Church Music in York 1770-1840.*

Watkins, Susan, *Jane Austen's Town and Country Style.*

Watson, J. Steven, *The Reign of George III.*

Willis, Ronald, *A Portrait of York.*

Willis, Ronald, *York As It Was.*

York Civic Trust, *Pyramids of Pleasure.*

York Chronicle.

York Courant.

York Herald.

Selected Index

Illustration Acknowledgements

Castle Museum, York: pages 13, 16, 22, 23, 25, 42, 43, 47, 72 and front cover – by kind permission.

Regimental Museum of the Prince of Wales' Own Regiment of Yorkshire, Tower Street, York: pages 13 and 56 – by kind permission.

W. Sessions Ltd (redrawing by J. B. Blackwell): p. 54.

J. Smith Coin and Stamp Shop, The Shambles, York: page 59 – by kind permission.

York Corporation (The Assembly Rooms): page 35 – by kind permission.

Yorkshire Architectural and York Archaeological Society's Evelyn Slide Collection: pages 11, 18, 27, 36, 52, 73 – by kind permission.

Antiquities of York, Henry Cave, 1813: pages 7, 63, 76.

History and Description of the ancient City of York, William Hargrove, 1818: pages frontispiece, 8, 12, 60, 69.

Thomas Bewick and his School, 1800 woodcuts, The Dover Pictorial Archive Series, 1962: pages 49, 70, 77.

The Old Coaching Days in Yorkshire, Tom Bradley, 1899: pages 72, 75.